T0322456

This brand-new book from the author of the bestselling *Fusing Fabrics* takes a new look at the creative potential of the fine-tipped soldering iron, a simple instrument that has revolutionized textile art. Author Margaret Beal, who is well-known as a pioneer of these techniques, takes you through the key methods of cutting, bonding and mark-making, and then expands on the various new ways you can use the soldering iron, particularly when using new synthetic materials such as Evolon, Lutradur and polymetallic fabrics.

Many traditional embroidery and sewing techniques have been the inspiration for Margaret's latest ideas, and some of the techniques discussed use the principles of drawn-thread work, insertions, patchwork, seams and layering. She has developed new and challenging approaches by experimenting with a variety of synthetic fabrics, creating new textures, distorting surfaces, and combining and manipulating these to form three-dimensional pieces.

The author gives detailed instructions on all the techniques, and the book is illustrated with a beautiful display of some of the most exciting textile art being made today.

New ideas in fusing fabric

New ideas in fusing fabric

Margaret Beal

BATSFORD

Acknowledgements

Lots of thanks to Andrew and Jo for all the help and encouragement they've given me while I've been working on this book, to Mark and Tracey for cutting all the fabric ready for me to use, and to Michael Wicks and Richard Dawson for the beautiful photography.

Last but not least, thank you to all those fellow embroiderers who bought my first book and encouraged me to write this one.

First published in the United Kingdom in 2013 by
Batsford
43 Great Ormond Street
London
WC1N 3HZ

An imprint of Pavilion Books Company Ltd

ISBN 978 1 84994 092 4

A CIP catalogue for this book is available from the British Library.

22 21 20 19 18
10 9 8 7 6 5 4 3 2

Reproduction by Rival Colour Ltd, UK
Printed and bound by Toppan Leefung Printing Ltd, China

This book can be ordered direct from the publisher at www.pavilionbooks.com, or try your local bookshop.

Distributed in the United States and Canada by Sterling Publishing Co., 387 Park Avenue South, New York, NY 10016, USA

CONTENTS

INTRODUCTION

I wrote my first book, Fusing Fabric, in 2005, introducing the reader to creative new textile techniques using a fine-tipped soldering iron on synthetic fabrics. Some of the great feedback resulting from that book has encouraged me to write a follow-up, so here it is.

For those of you who have never used a soldering iron on fabric, this book covers the three basic techniques of cutting, fusing and mark-making on synthetic fabric. You will also find many suggestions for using these techniques and pointers to the easiest fabrics to use for perfect results.

For those of you who are very familiar with the techniques, I have been working on new ideas and ways of using them and have described in detail the steps involved in creating many of the pieces featured here. Some of them you will find easier than others. There is a certain amount of trial and error involved, so the outcome of your work will probably not be exactly the same as mine, but if you give yourself time to experiment with the techniques and use a variety of different fabrics, you will get to know instinctively which fabric works best for the technique you are using.

New Ideas in Fusing Fabric is full of new work inspired by my love of traditional embroidery and sewing techniques. Taking these as starting points, I have tried to convey my design process and how I create new work. For example, a running-stitch mark can be used for basting, layering, quilting, appliqué or for marking a design on fabric. A seam can become raised and undulating or have loops and motifs fused between the layers to create an intricately patterned raised surface. A simple shape can be manipulated to create a three-dimensional form.

There are many ways in which the techniques could be used, including textile art, fashion, jewellery, millinery, home furnishing or hobbies such as card-making. I hope you will enjoy experimenting and adapting them to use in your own creative way.

Running the soldering iron along the edge of a mirror plate to make a mark on fabric.

Basic tools and equipment

Those of you familiar with my first book will already know all about the basic tools and equipment, but there are one or two important reminders and additions, so it would be worth your while reading the following list.

Soldering iron

In order to cut, fuse and make very sharp marks on the fabric, you need a soldering iron with an extremely fine tip; the one I use is an 18-watt model with a tip that looks like a well-sharpened pencil. It takes three or four minutes to reach its full heat, but once hot it stays at the same temperature until switched off. The tip eventually wears down, but can be replaced. Angled fine-pointed tips are also available. See Suppliers, page 126.

Fine wire wool

To keep the tip of the soldering iron clean, you need a very fine wire wool, grade 0000.

Soldering iron, face mask and wire wool.

Metal rulers

A metal ruler plays a very important part in the cutting and fusing process because, when pressed on the fabrics, it prevents them slipping out of position. It also ensures that there is good contact between layers of fabric, as it leaves no air between them.

A mirror plate makes an invaluable short ruler. It is especially useful for putting pressure on layered fabrics in the precise place where you are scoring short lines or making running-stitch marks or other marks. I use one all the time and recommend you make one of these part of your basic tool kit. A short smooth-edged metal ruler serves the same purpose, and is ideal for most other methods. Fancy-edged metal rulers or paper-tearers are also useful.

Rulers and templates.

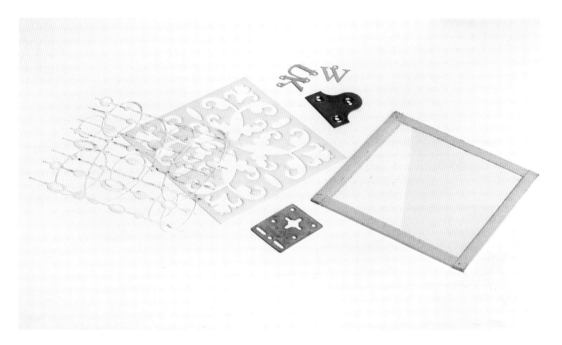

Plastic and metal templates, mirror plate and glass.

Cardboard templates, sticky-backed card shapes and printing block.

Glass

You will need to work on a piece of ordinary picture glass, A4-size or larger. To avoid cutting yourself, cover the edges with masking tape.

Soldering iron stand

I use an upturned terracotta flowerpot; the tip of the soldering iron sits safely in the drainage hole, with the handle sticking up.

Protective face mask

Because of the risk of inhaling toxic fumes from melting fabric, it is advisable to wear a protective face mask or respirator and to work in a well ventilated room. I personally try not to use fabrics that give off very strong odours.

Health and safety

- Obviously, the soldering iron is very hot and will give you a nasty burn if you are careless with it.
- Always wear a face mask or respirator for protection from breathing in any possibly harmful fumes, and work in a well ventilated room.
- Be careful not have any cables or leads on your work surface that could be damaged by the hot tip of the soldering iron.
- Use fine wire wool, grade 0000, to keep the tip of the soldering iron clean, but never use it as a rest for the soldering iron, because it could go up in flames.
- Cover the sharp edges of the glass with masking tape.
- Remember to switch the soldering iron off when you have finished using it.

Hints and tips

- The word 'cut' always means cut with the soldering iron, unless otherwise stated.
- Whenever I say 'use the ruler', wherever possible always use the mirror plate, because it's practical and you can work faster than with an ordinary ruler.
- For making quick, short marks, try to use the tip of your fingernail for putting pressure on a precise area instead of the mirror plate. This will help you work even more quickly.
- Remember to clean the tip of the soldering iron with fine wire wool and to clean the edge of metal rulers and templates now and again.
- Always clean the tip of the soldering iron before switching it off; it's much easier to clean a hot tip than one with solidified melted fabric stuck to it.
- Rub the surface of the glass over with the wire wool now and again to get rid of any tiny bits of fabric that may have stuck to it; you should also wash the glass occasionally.
- When working on a dark work surface, put a sheet of white paper under the glass so that you can clearly see the colours of the fabrics you're working with.
- Put a cutting mat or lined paper under the glass if you want to score accurate lines on the fabric.
- The respirator will make a temporary indentation on your face. I recommend that you stop working three hours before going to a social event, because the marks disappear rather slowly!
- Throughout the methods described in this book, I suggest using a range of synthetic fabrics, which all behave differently and take a little practice to get to grips with. If you're new to using the soldering iron, it would be best to use nylon organza to begin with, until you feel more confident with the technique. You can then experiment with a range of synthetic fabrics.
- Often, just running the tip of the soldering iron at a different angle, or more slowly, will prevent the fabric from being dragged.
- If you need to run the tip of the soldering iron along the edge of the ruler or around a template a second time, always run it in the same direction; don't be tempted to run it backwards and forwards or the edge of the fabric will become very messy.

Threads

Whether you stitch by machine or hand, always use a natural thread, such as cotton, silk or good quality rayon, because these won't melt if they come into contact with the soldering iron.

Always test a thread before using it by holding it under tension on the glass and running the tip of the soldering iron across it two or three times. If it melts and cuts in half, don't use it.

Synthetic threads

Snippets of meltable thread can be sandwiched between two pieces of synthetic fabric and used for many of the techniques in this book.

Nylon and polyester organza fabrics.

Fabrics

For cutting, fusing and making marks, you need to use synthetic fabrics that will melt with the heat of the soldering iron.

Testing fabrics

Always test fabrics before using them to make sure that they are entirely synthetic, not a mixture of synthetic and natural fibres.
To test a fabric, place it on the glass and run the tip of the soldering iron across both the warp and the weft; it should melt and cut easily with no resistance.

Nylon or polyester organza

If you have never used a soldering iron on fabric before, there is no doubt that these very lightweight transparent fabrics are the easiest ones with which to practise before you start experimenting with other synthetics.

Other suitable synthetic fabrics

If you are very familiar with the techniques, try using some of the fabrics listed below. If you find that some of them tend to drag as you run the tip of the soldering iron along the edge of the ruler or around a template, the solution is to stabilize them by backing them with a piece of nylon organza or by interleaving them between layers.

Many of the techniques use lots of plain fabrics just to create depth. I often use synthetic scarves that have been given to me or that I've bought from charity shops. The plain or uninteresting ones I use to create depth for base layers, keeping more interesting ones for top layers.

List of suitable fabrics

- Nylon or polyester organza.
- Polyester taffeta and brocade ribbons.
- Habotai polyester.
- Polyester satin.
- Vilene (Pellon)   available in various weights (I use S80/239).
- Lutradur – a non-woven white polyester fabric, which is available in various weights (I mainly use 130).
- Evolon – a non-woven white fabric made from polyester and nylon, which feels like very soft chamois leather and is available in two weights (I use the lighter weight).
- Sizoflor – a semi-transparent, thin, stiff fabric, made from long strands of enmeshed fibres and available in a wide range of colours.
- Acrylic felt.
- Polyester metallic fabric, also known as polyester metallic gauze.

Other fabrics suitable for use with a soldering iron.

1 CUTTING, FUSING AND TEMPLATES

Cutting, fusing and making marks on synthetic fabrics are the three basic techniques described here. If you are new to these techniques, I recommend that you start by using nylon organza for making seams and cutting motifs. For fusing fabrics or motifs to a base layer, I suggest that you use either acrylic felt or two or three layers of black polyester lining fabric. Those readers who are very familiar with the techniques might like to start experimenting with a range of synthetic fabrics.

Sometimes, you may have problems when fusing very flimsy lightweight fabrics together: for example, the fabric may drag as you run the tip of the iron along the edge of the ruler. If this happens, try interleaving pieces of nylon organza between the layers. Alternatively, just running the tip of the iron along the edge of the ruler either at a different angle or more slowly may prevent the fabric from dragging.

When you run the tip of the soldering iron along the edge of a metal ruler or around a metal template, it will cut the fabric, going right through to the glass. If you use two or more layers of fabric, it will cut through all of them and at the same time fuse all the edges together. It's important that you put sufficient pressure on the ruler or template to ensure that there is good contact between the layers and prevent them from slipping about.

You can cut out shapes and fuse fabrics together freehand, but the edges will not be as well fused or as neat as when using the ruler or a template. As you become more confident with these techniques, however, you will find that it is quicker to use the tip of your fingernail to put pressure on the fabrics instead of the ruler (or mirror plate) when making quick short marks.

Once you know how to join two pieces of fabric together with a seam, to fuse layers of fabric together, to cut out shapes and to make marks on fabric, you will realize that all of the methods described in this book are just combinations and manipulations of these basic techniques. There are no secrets: it's just a matter of practice, but I recommend that you read through a method before you start, just as you would when reading a recipe.

Shapes cut out from layered fabrics were fused to a backing made from fabrics felted together using the Embellisher machine, which was also used around the edges and over some areas of the shapes. Lastly, the shapes were edged with strong marks made with the tip of the soldering iron.

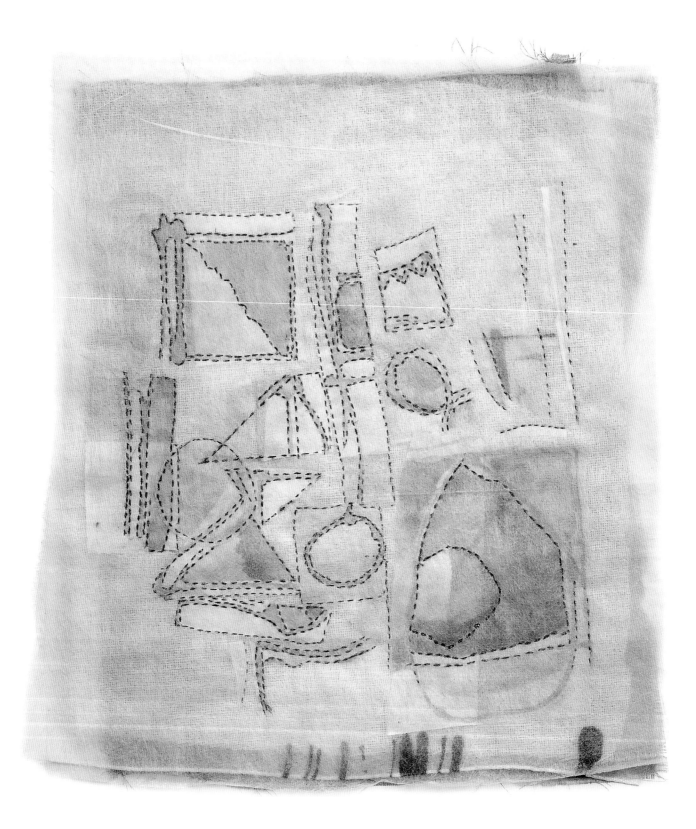

Shapes were cut from a polyester scarf then arranged on three layers of fabric and covered with a lightweight transparent fabric known as Zeelon. Running-stitch marks were made around the edges of the shapes to fuse them to the backing fabric.

Fusing with running stitches

I have started with the running-stitch mark, as it is used in so many of the techniques and methods throughout the book and can be used just for practicalities or decoratively. The method below describes how to fuse two or more layers of fabric permanently together. It can also be used to just very lightly baste layers together while planning the layout of a piece of work. If you subsequently change your mind, the fabrics can easily be pulled apart.

Requirements

- Basic tools and equipment (remember that a mirror plate makes an ideal short ruler)
- Lightweight non-stretch synthetic fabrics (if you are new to this technique I recommend nylon organza)

Method

To make very neat sharp marks that will permanently fuse layers of fabric together, it's always best to use the edge of the ruler. This helps you to put pressure on the fabrics so that there is good contact between the layers, preventing them from moving or slipping about.

1. Layer two or more pieces of your chosen fabric on the glass, one on top of the other.
2. Place the ruler horizontally on the fabrics, approximately 1cm (½in) below the top edge, and run the tip of the soldering iron along it to score a row of short straight marks through the layers, fusing them together.

For speed, it is possible to make the running-stitch mark very lightly as you run the tip along the edge of the ruler. You can then easily pull the fabrics apart if you decide to reposition them. You can also make marks without using the ruler: the secret is to press the tip of your fingernail firmly on the layers, and then make the mark as close as possible to it, without singeing the tip of your fingernail.

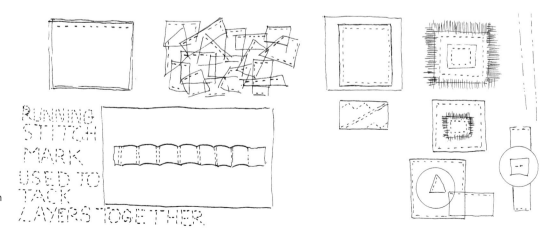

Using the running-stitch mark to fuse shapes to a backing fabric.

Using templates to cut motifs and shapes

Once again, if you have never used this technique before, begin by using three to four layers of nylon organza, before trying a variety of other lightweight, non-stretch polyester fabrics.

Requirements

- Basic tools and equipment
- Nylon organza
- A variety of light- to medium-weight polyester fabrics (non-stretch) and one or two layers of polyester lining fabric with which to back them
- Flat metal templates, such as squares, diamonds and circles, in various sizes

Tip

Remember to clean the tip of the soldering iron regularly with fine wire wool.

Warning

Some metal templates might get a little bit hot, so be careful.

Method

1. Layer one or two pieces of polyester lining fabric on the glass, with one or two layers of lightweight polyester fabric on top.
2. Place the ruler horizontally on the fabrics, about 1cm (½ in) below the top edge, and run the tip of the soldering iron along the edge to score a row of running-stitch marks, basting the fabrics together.
3. Hold a template firmly on the fabrics and run the tip of the soldering iron all around the edge at a fairly upright angle, making sure you cut right through to the glass. The shape should then pop out easily.
4. Experiment with the different types of fabric and the number of layers you use. Scoring fine lines over the layers before you cut around the template will help to stabilize very flimsy fabrics, and can also be decorative. To do this, tilt and press the edge of the ruler or a template on the layers and run the tip of the soldering iron along the edge, taking care not to score right through to the glass.

Note

When using very lightweight flimsy fabrics, you may have difficulty cutting shapes with neat, sharp edges, or find that the fabric drags as you run the tip of the soldering iron around the template. Interleaving a piece of nylon organza between the base layers will help to prevent this.

Motifs cut from a variety of layered fabrics, some with fine lines scored over them.

Crinkly-edged shapes

When making shapes with crinkly edges, it's worth experimenting with a variety of polyester fabrics, to see how differently they behave, and varying the number of layers you use.

Requirements

- Basic tools and equipment
- Two pieces of nylon organza
- Two pieces of lightweight polyester fabric, patterned or plain
- A geometric metal template

Method

1. Sandwich the two pieces of nylon organza between the other two fabrics and place them on the glass.
2. Hold and press the template very firmly on the fabrics and run the tip of the soldering iron at an upright angle around the edge, cutting right through to the glass.
3. Being very careful not to burn your fingers, hold the resulting shape off the glass and run the tip of the soldering iron slowly all around the edges of the shape. Do so in one continuous movement, for as long as possible, and then clean the tip and carry on. The edges will shrink, causing the shape to become slightly dished. A build-up of melted fabric will solidify on the edges, forming a dark, crinkly border. Use your fingers to persuade the edges and corners to curl up, at the same time running the tip around the edges two or three times more, to make them curl up even more and become darker still.

Crinkly-edged shapes made with a variety of fabrics.

Cutting shapes from multiple layers of fabric

The more layers you use for this technique, the slower you will move the tip of the soldering iron around the edge of the template. Be aware that the templates might therefore get very hot, so you will need to take extra care.

First test the fabrics to make sure they are all entirely synthetic. Do this by running the tip of the soldering iron across both the warp and the weft to see if they melt and cut easily.

If you have any problem cutting easily and neatly through the layers because the fabric drags as you run the tip of the soldering iron along the ruler, interleaving a piece of nylon organza between some of the layers should solve the problem.

It is to possible cut through up to eight, nine, ten or more layers of fabric, depending on their thickness. These do not all have to be particularly interesting-looking fabrics, as most of them will be sandwiched between the two outer layers.

Requirements
- Basic tools and equipment
- Medium or lightweight fabrics
- Two interesting fabrics for the top and bottom layers
- A metal template

Method
1. Layer plain fabrics between two interesting-looking ones and place them on the glass.
2. Hold and press the template very firmly on the fabrics, making sure that they won't slip or move and that there is good contact between the layers. Position the tip of the soldering iron at the edge at a very upright angle and slowly move the tip all around. Try to do this in as continuous a movement as possible to obtain a smooth, clean-cut edge; all the layers will fuse together and the shape will pop out. The surface of the shapes will have a soft, cushion-like feel, because there will still be a certain amount of air trapped between the layers.

Scoring fine lines on the shape will flatten and harden the surface and the colour of the fabric beneath will show through. To do this, rest the edge of the ruler (the mirror plate is the best thing to use here) firmly on a shape. Run the tip of the soldering iron along at a shallow angle and score fine lines, one under the other, cutting deep into the layers, but not right through to the glass. At this stage, if you crinkle the edges, they will shrink and become slightly dish-shaped (see previous method for crinkly-edged shapes on page 20).

Further suggestion
You could score the lines on the layered fabrics either before, or both before and after, you cut out the shapes.

Shapes cut from layered fabric and finished with crinkly edges; three shapes have been layered on top of one another and stitched together.

Shapes cut from nine layers of fabric, with fine lines scored over them and finished with crinkly edges.

Cutting shapes with intricately patterned surfaces

After cutting out shapes from layered fabrics, you're left with lots of fabric with negative shapes cut into them. If you layer these and place them on a backing of two pieces of nylon organza, then maybe add a few motifs or strips on top, you can use the resulting fabric for cutting out shapes with intricately patterned surfaces. You will, of course, be left with another piece with negative shapes, which you can then use again.

First test the fabrics to make sure they are all entirely synthetic. Do this by running the tip of the soldering iron across both the warp and the weft to see if they melt and cut easily.

Further suggestion
You can also fuse painted Bondaweb (Wonder Under) onto layered motifs (for example in the piece shown at the bottom of page 125).

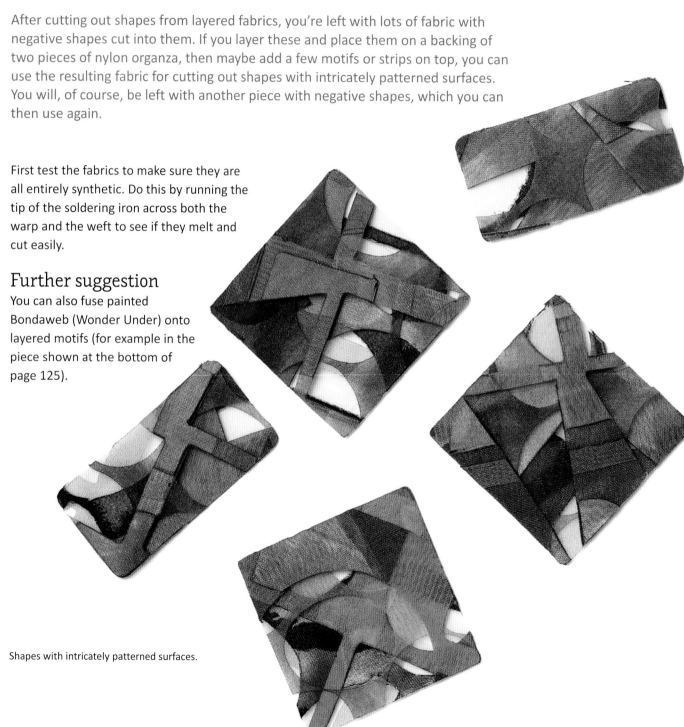

Shapes with intricately patterned surfaces.

Fusing shapes to a backing fabric

The secret of fusing shapes to a backing fabric and leaving scarcely a mark showing is to run the tip of the soldering iron along the very edge, using the minimum of pressure.

Method

1. Using templates, cut out some shapes and arrange them on a backing fabric.
2. Align the edge of the ruler with the very edge of a shape, so that you can hardly see any of the shape peeping out from beneath.
3. Angle the tip of the soldering iron in towards the edge of ruler and run it, with the minimum of pressure, along the base of the shape. For heavyweight shapes, you need to run the tip slowly and you may have to repeat the action to be sure the shape is firmly fused to the backing. You could also try holding the shapes firmly in position with your fingers instead of using the ruler.

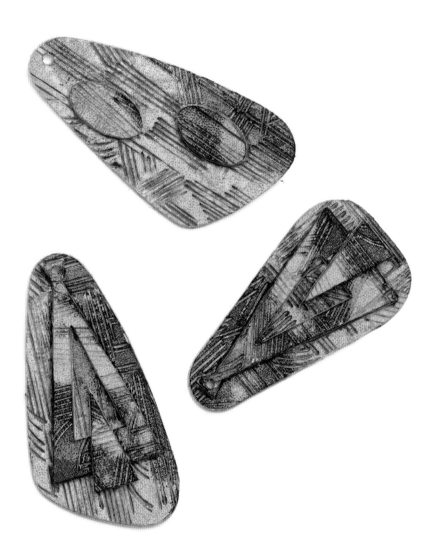

Shapes cut from layered fabrics scored with fine lines, then layered and fused together by running the tip of the soldering iron around the edges.

Brooches

The decorative elements of these brooches were made using a variety of fabrics. Some have been dyed or foiled, or have snippets of glitzy fabric fused onto them.

Styles

The heart-shaped brooches were made from snippets of organza and foil layered onto lamé or nylon organza, fused to Lutradur, scored with lines and patterns, and then decorated with hand stitching and beads.

The rectangular brooch was made from Anaglypta wallpaper, which was painted, dried, foiled and overlaid with organza, then backed with Lutradur and hand-stitched to accentuate the raised areas.

For the silver shield-shaped brooch, Anaglypta wallpaper was painted, dried and foiled, and then overlaid with clear PVC and decorated with hand stitching.

To make the heart-shaped brooch with floral motif, dyed Lutradur was ironed over with Transfoil. The Lutradur just picks up flecks when there's no Bondaweb (Wonder Under). It was then decorated with twisted wire and beads.

The small teardrop-shaped brooch was made from a glitzy fabric overlaid with organza and iridescent film and decorated with hand stitching and beads.

Brooches made by Christine Thomas.

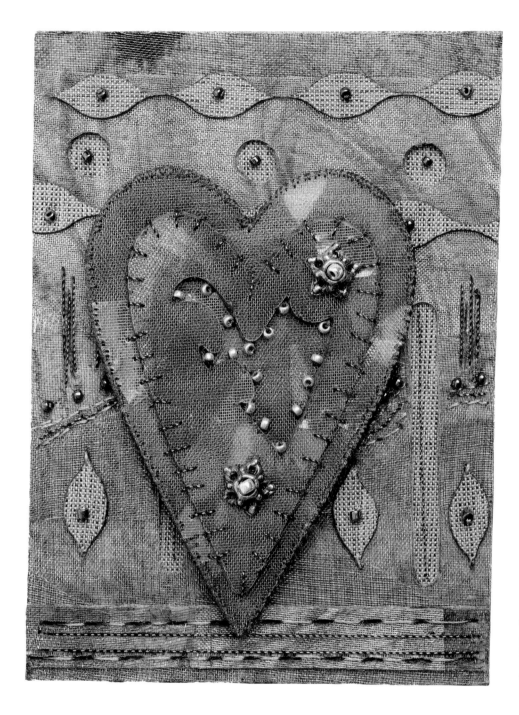

The large heart brooch placed against a fused background fabric. Brooch by Christine Thomas.

Making up the brooches

The prepared top layer of fabric is laid out onto a piece of 100/130 Lutradur for stability. The main shapes are then cut out by running the soldering iron round the edge of the template, and some of the smaller shapes are cut freehand. All the cut edges are then coloured with watercolour pencils. The smaller shapes are layered and fused onto the main shape and embellished with marks and hand stitching. When all the decorative elements are finished, a backing is cut from Vilene backed with a coordinating faux-silk fabric, and the brooch is attached to it with tiny overcast stitching all around the edge.

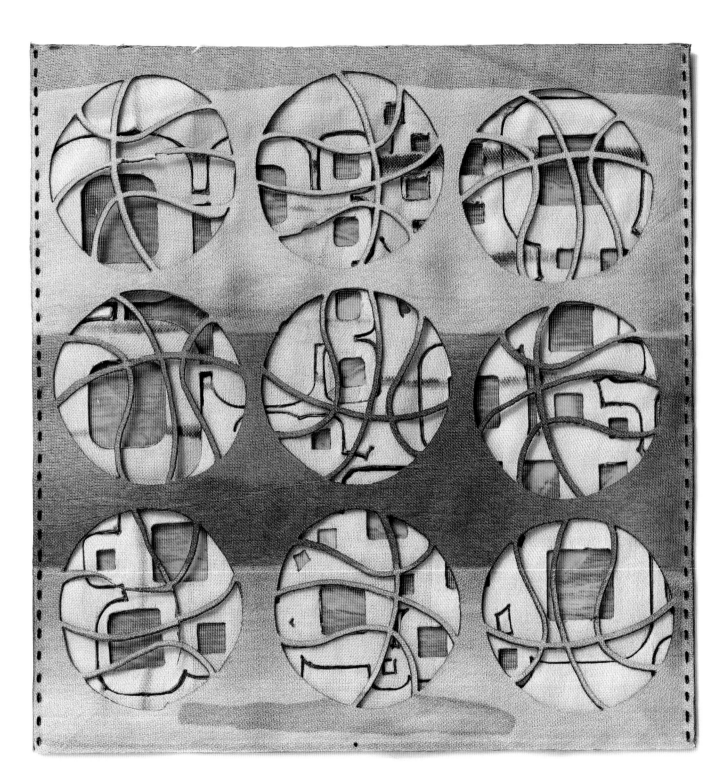

Cutting out shapes using templates and taking five layers
of fabric for both the top and bottom layers. Bottom layer:
shapes cut using a cardboard template; top layer: shapes
cut using a metal template.

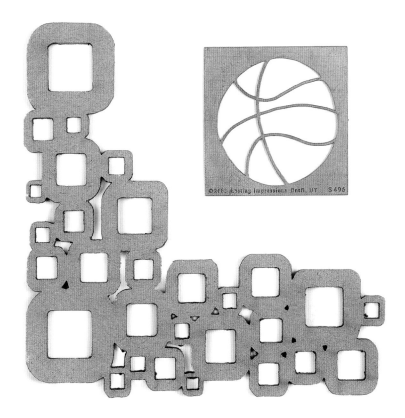

Metal and cardboard templates.

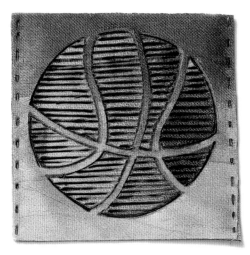

The top sample shows the negative areas left after removing cut shapes. The centre shows the same sample put onto a backing fabric, the shapes replaced with some of them scored with fine lines. The bottom sample shows a contrasting colour sample, with all the positive shapes scored with fine lines.

Using stencils to fuse motifs to a backing fabric

This method works best with lightweight motifs or shapes. It's important to have a nice fine tip on the soldering iron.

Requirements
- Basic tools and equipment
- For the backing, three pieces of nylon organza and one piece of lightweight polyester fabric
- Motifs cut from layered fabrics
- Small metal stencils or templates

Method
1. Layer the nylon on the glass, with the polyester on top.
2. Place a motif on top and position the stencil shape or template so that it sits in the centre. Next, run the tip of the soldering iron around the edge, cutting right through to the glass; the motif will be fused firmly in place.

Motifs fused to a backing using stencils and templates.

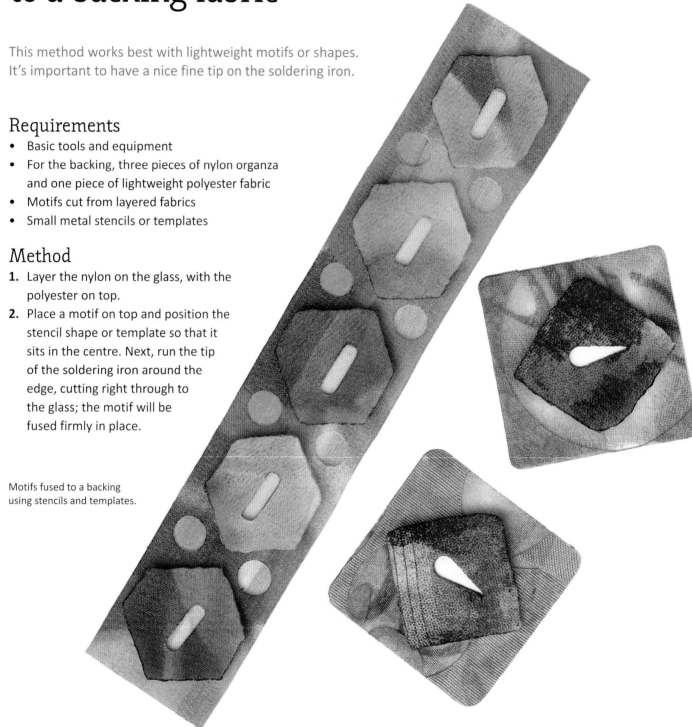

Decorative fusing with running-stitch marks

Highly visible running-stitch marks can be used to fuse motifs, shapes or a finished piece of work to a backing fabric. The marks will be clearly visible and are intended to be decorative as well as practical.

Method

1. Arrange the shapes on a backing of two or three layers of polyester fabric.
2. Tilt and press the narrow edge of the ruler on the outer edge of each shape and score very visible running-stitch marks all around the edge, working into the layers beneath.

These shapes were cut both freehand and using templates, then fused to a backing of layered polyester fabrics using running-stitch marks.

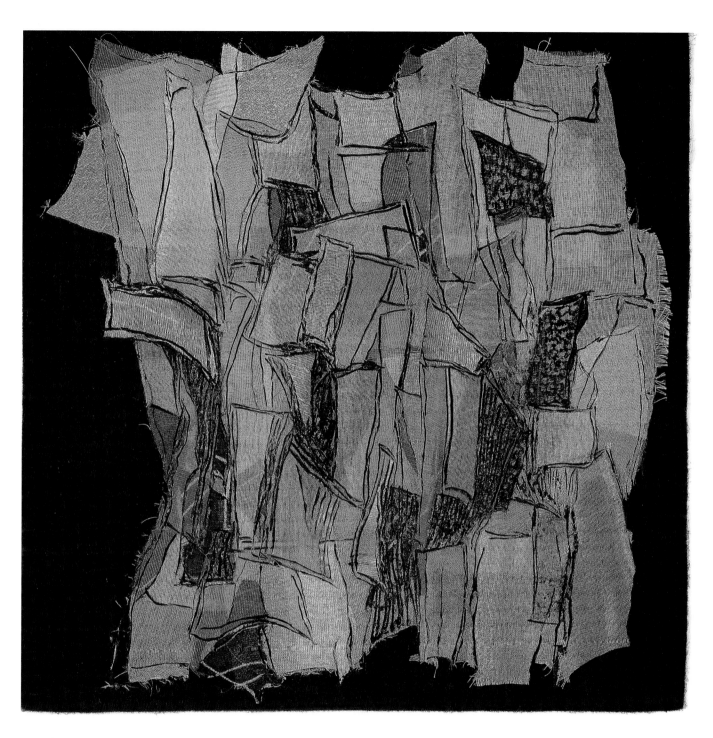

Random shapes were cut with scissors and then
layered and fused to a backing of acrylic felt with
lightly-scored running-stitch marks. The marks
were then drawn into freehand, to make a
continuous strong mark all around the edge.

Layered strips and shapes with motifs cut out and
then repositioned and fused with scored lines and
patterns to a backing of acrylic felt.

Fusing lightweight shapes or motifs to a backing with running-stitch marks

For this technique, lightweight shapes are fused to a backing by making running-stitch marks around the edge of a template.

Method

1. Place a shape on a backing formed from two or three layers of fabric. Place the template you used to cut it out exactly in position back on top of your shape.
2. Press hard on the template and make evenly spaced and very short running-stitch marks with the tip of the soldering iron all around the edge; the tip just catches the edge of the shape enough to fuse it down. A tiny dot won't fuse the layers together firmly; it has to be a very short running-stitch mark.

Further suggestion

For the backing fabric, use a firm acrylic felt in a dark colour. Follow the method described left, but score a continuous mark into the felt instead of the running stitches, running it all around the edge of the template.

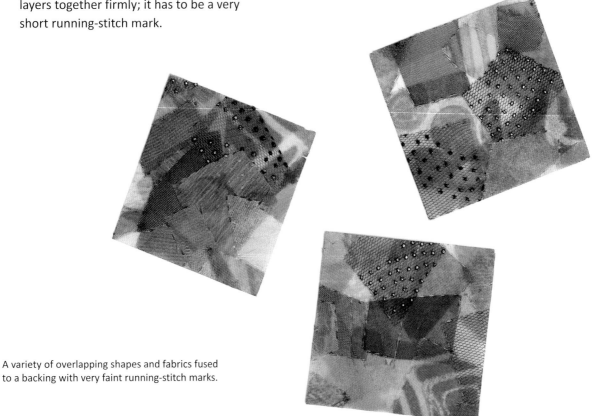

A variety of overlapping shapes and fabrics fused to a backing with very faint running-stitch marks.

Fusing shapes to a backing with running-stitch marks
made around the edge of the template.

Shapes were fused to a backing with a continuous line
scored around the edge of each. The piece is cut to size
and fused to acrylic felt with running-stitch marks
scored around the border.

To fuse a finished piece of work to a backing fabric

Simply place the work on the backing fabric and position the metal ruler 1cm (½ in) in from the edge, then run the tip of the soldering iron around all four sides, cutting right through to the glass.

The intricate pattern was cut using a metal bookmark as a template. It has been fused to a backing of two layers of polyester organza.

Die-cut cardboard templates

Card or chipboard letter shapes are very useful for lettering and can be bought from most craft shops. The fabric sticks to the edge of the card, which makes the shapes very rigid, but you can peel the fabric off if you want to.

Requirements

- Basic tools and equipment
- Two layers of medium-weight interesting or decorative fabric for the top layers (I used two layers of a polyester metallic fabric, also known as polyester tissue)
- Five layers of acetate fabric, for the base
- Card or chipboard alphabet shapes (these are usually quite thick)

Method

1. Layer the interesting fabrics on the glass with the acetate fabrics on top. Baste all the layers together with a row of running-stitch marks, made just below the top edge.
2. Place the letter shape back to front on the fabrics, so that the letter will be facing the right way when you have finished the cutting and turned it over.
3. Score a border of running-stitch marks, about 1cm (½ in) away from the letter, to prevent the fabrics from moving.
4. Holding it very upright, run the tip of the soldering iron slowly around the edge of the letter, so that it really hugs the edge of the card.

Upper-case letters of the alphabet cut using die-cut card shapes and lower-case letters cut using sticky-backed thin card shapes.

Using sticky-backed alphabet shapes

A slightly different method is used for sticky-backed shapes made from thin card.

Requirements

- Basic tools and equipment
- Two layers of decorative fabric
- Three layers of acetate lining fabric
- Die-cut sticky-backed alphabet shapes
- One piece of nylon organza

Method

1. Layer the interesting fabrics on the glass with the acetate fabrics on top. Baste all the layers together with a row of running-stitch marks, made just below the top edge.
2. Peel the letters off the card and press them firmly onto the nylon organza.
3. Turn the nylon over and place it on the layered fabric so that the letters are now facing you back to front. Run the tip of the soldering iron around the edge of the letters right through to the glass, and the shapes will pop out.

Die-cut cardboard templates and shapes cut from layered grids (leftovers after cutting out lots of squares and rectangles).

Mark-making on gesso-coated nylon organza on a backing of black acrylic felt – the letters were fused down by running the tip of the soldering iron very carefully around the base of the shape. Design by Jo Beal.

Fusing a cardboard template to the fabric

Here I explain how to fuse a cardboard template to a backing of layered fabrics so that the shape stands out in high relief. This does take a bit of practice, but I think it is worth the effort.

Requirements

- Basic tools and equipment
- Die-cut card or chipboard shape
- Paints or crayons, to colour the shapes
- Five or six pieces of acetate lining fabric
- Nylon organza
- One decorative polyester fabric

Warning

Read the health and safety warnings concerning any harmful fumes that may be given off by paints or crayons when they come into contact with heat. Make sure you wear your mask.

Method

1. Colour the cardboard shape with paint or crayons and leave it to dry.
2. Lay five or six layers of fabric, one on top of the other, to create sufficient depth to ensure that the tip of the soldering iron won't go right through to the glass when used at a shallow angle. Place a piece of nylon organza on top and finish with the decorative, colourful fabric on top of that.
3. Baste all the layers together by scoring a row of running-stitch marks, made horizontally along the edge of the ruler, about 1cm (½ in) down from the top.
4. Place the cardboard shape on the fabric.
5. Starting with all the most intricate areas, such as swirls and curves, hold and press firmly on the shape with your fingers. Rest the tip of the soldering iron in towards the base of the shape, making sure that it hugs the side of the card, and then run it at a shallow angle. Do this carefully, a bit at a time, taking it slowly around the edge. If the tip goes right through to the glass, put another piece of fabric underneath the layers. The fibres of the card will stick to the fabric and the card will stay in place as long as you are careful to keep the finished piece flat.

Die-cut cardboard template, painted and fused onto
layered fabrics. Close-up shown left.

Using an image on paper as a template

You can use a photocopied image of one of your own designs or a copyright-free image from a book or magazine. This method also leaves you with lovely negative shapes, which can be layered and fused to a backing fabric of a contrasting colour.

Requirements
- Basic tools and equipment
- A photocopied image or photocopy of your own design
- One piece of nylon organza (I used black nylon organza)
- A medium-sized tapestry needle
- Two or three pieces of nylon organza for the backing fabric

Here a figure has been fused onto a backing of nylon organza that was first coated with gesso.

Method
1. Place the photocopy on the glass and cover it with a piece of nylon organza.
2. To prevent the fabric from moving, fuse it to the paper with a row of running-stitch marks, made horizontally, 2cm (a scant 1in) down from the top of the fabric.
3. Stretch your fingers firmly on the fabric over the area of the design you are working on, to keep it taut and to prevent air pockets forming between the fabric and the paper.
4. Little by little, follow the outline of the shape with the tip of the soldering iron, as if you were tracing the line with a pencil; you do not have to press very hard. The fabric will cut and the cut edge will stick to the paper. Try not to disturb anything until you've finished all the cutting, because this will make it much easier to cut accurately.
5. When all the cutting is finished, very carefully tease the excess fabric around the shape off the paper. The shape itself will probably be very well stuck to the paper, so break the seal carefully by pushing the tip of the tapestry needle between it and the paper and then working it carefully all the way around the edge.
6. Layer the backing fabrics on the glass, one on top of the other; baste them together with a row of running-stitch marks, made horizontally, about 1cm (½in) down from the top,
7. Place the shape on the backing fabric and spread your fingers over it so that it can't possibly move. Next, with the tip of the soldering iron angled sideways onto it, little by little, quickly and very lightly stroke the outer edge a tiny bit at a time to fuse it to the backing. In some areas, you may find it easier to press the tip of your fingernail as close as possible to the tip of the soldering iron to maintain the pressure on the shape.
8. Being careful not to cut right through to the glass, score extremely fine lines very quickly and lightly down to the bottom of the shape.

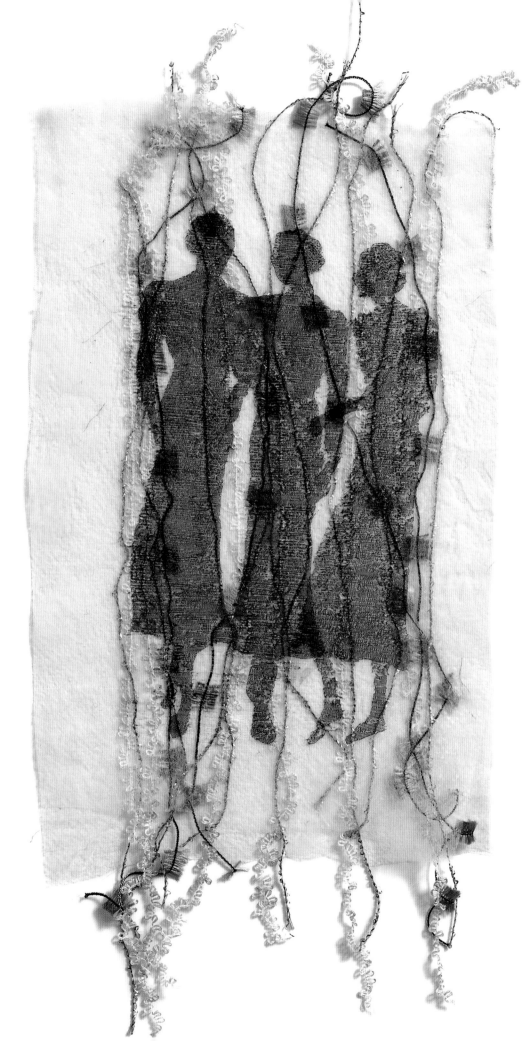

For the backing fabric, I layered strands of textured synthetic yarn between two pieces of very thin, cheap polyester garden fleece on a base of nylon organza. I then covered the layers with parchment paper and ironed over it. The fleece fused lightly to the yarns, but when the organza figures were fused on top, and scored very lightly with fine lines, all the layers fused together very well.

2 SEAMS, RIBBONS AND BATONS

Once you know how to make a seam, you can develop the technique to make intricate patchwork pieces. Strips and ribbons can be fused to a backing to create a whole piece that in turn can be cut into shapes using templates.

Strips cut from many layers of fabric can be as rigid as matchsticks, and, depending on your imagination, could be used for all sorts of effects in addition to the flower shapes and spokes you see here.

Fusing batons together to form a circle of spokes. The spokes were manipulated and the ends fused together to form complete circular flower shapes, which were then stitched to a backing of printed Vilene (Pellon).

To make a seam

Seams will lie in different ways depending on the type of fabric you use. For example, if you use nylon organza and the tip of your soldering iron is very fine, the finished seam will be almost invisible and will lie very flat, though if you run your finger along the back of the seam you will feel a slight ridge. If you use a soft, flimsy polyester fabric, the seam will not lie flat and the finished surface will form into raised, soft folds. If you want the surface to lie flat, you need to back the flimsy polyester fabric with a piece of nylon organza first. A soft raised surface, alternating with a flat surface, will be formed when you make a seam joining a firm or rigid fabric with a soft flimsy polyester fabric.

Requirements

- Basic tools and equipment
- Strips of nylon organza and/or a variety of lightweight polyester fabrics, about 5 x 15cm (2 x 6in)

If you've never made a seam using the soldering iron, I suggest you use only nylon organza to begin with before trying out other fabrics. If you are more experienced, experiment with a variety of fabrics to create some of the surfaces listed above.

Method

1. Layer two strips of fabric, of contrasting colours, on the glass, one on top of the other, aligning them at the top edge.
2. Place the ruler horizontally on the fabrics, about 5mm (a scant ¼ in) from the top, and run the tip of the iron slowly along the edge, cutting right through to the glass. Don't be tempted to run the tip backwards and forwards or put the ruler too close to the edge of the fabrics, because the seam will be rough and messy if you do.
3. Leave the ruler in position while you lift the waste strip off the glass. If it doesn't lift off easily, perhaps the fabric is just stuck to the glass, so try again. Alternatively, it could be that you ran the iron too fast, in which case you will have to repeat the action.
4. Open out the fabrics and press gently along the seam with your finger; this is the right side of the work.
5. Take a third strip and align its top edge with the top edge of the work. Repeat steps 2, 3 and 4. Continue to fuse consecutive strips,

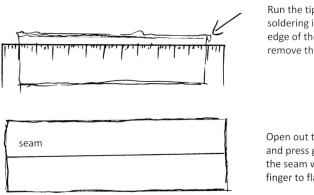

Run the tip of the soldering iron along the edge of the ruler then remove the waste strip.

Open out the fabrics and press gently along the seam with your finger to flatten it.

Seams made with a variety of fabrics – circular apertures have been cut out of the finished piece, which was then fused to two layers of nylon organza.

following steps 2, 3 and 4, until you've made a larger piece. Place it on the glass, right side up, with the seams facing you vertically.

6. If you have used only nylon organza, place the ruler on top horizontally and run the tip of the iron along it to cut the piece into strips varying in width between 3 and 6cm (1¼ and 2½ in). If you have used a variety of fabrics, it's easier to cut the strips with scissors.

7. If you have used only nylon organza, place one strip horizontally on the glass and place another on top, with right sides matching and aligning the top edges, but reversing the top strip so the colour order runs in the opposite direction to that of the strip underneath. Repeat steps 2, 3 and 4 and then move on to step 8. If you have used a variety of fabrics, the strips will not lie flat, so lay them on the glass with right sides matching and aligning the top edges. Next, place the ruler 5mm (a scant ¼ in) below the top and score a row of running-stitch marks along to baste the strips in position, and then place the ruler on the marks and continue with steps 2, 3 and 4, before moving on to step 8.

8. Cut the piece into strips again; make some new strips, and fuse them all together to make a whole piece.

Seams using rulers with fancy edges

Follow the method described on pages 46–47, but use a metal ruler or paper tearer with a wavy or zigzagged edge. The seam will form the same shape as the ruler and the finished surface will be raised.

Suggestion

Try making a seam joining a very rigid fabric, such as Lutradur or Sizoflor, to a flimsy polyester fabric.

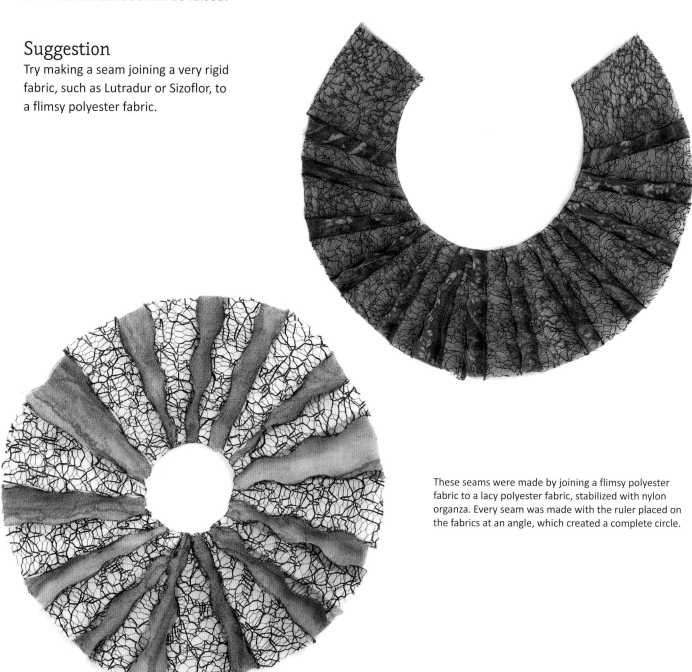

These seams were made by joining a flimsy polyester fabric to a lacy polyester fabric, stabilized with nylon organza. Every seam was made with the ruler placed on the fabrics at an angle, which created a complete circle.

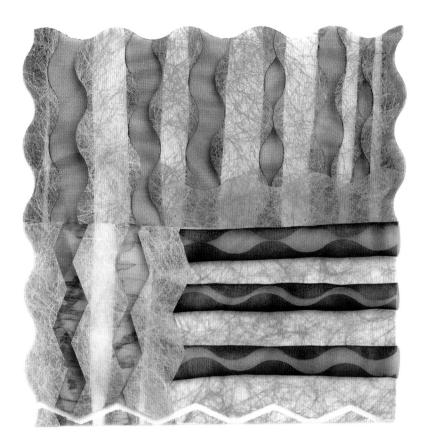

Sizoflor and a flimsy polyester fabric were fused together using fancy-edged rulers. The finished piece is backed onto Lutradur to support it.

I have carefully teased and withdrawn many of the weft threads within the polyester fabric in order to distort the pattern and make the fabric even lighter. The polyester fabric has formed a raised, very soft surface in contrast to the flat surface of the lightweight Lutradur. The piece is embellished with motifs cut from tea-stained Vilene, scored with singe marks.

Tip
Save the withdrawn threads and fuse them between two pieces of Bondaweb to make a lightweight fabric that could be used for many of the techniques in this book.

Fusing motifs within a seam

Motifs can easily be fused between seams.

Requirements
- Basic tools and equipment
- Nylon organza
- Metal templates (I used a coin)

Tip
Try making the running-stitch mark on the motif without using a metal ruler; this takes a bit of practice, but it's quicker. The secret is to ensure that there is good contact between the layers by pressing your fingernail on the motif and making the mark as close to the tip your fingernail as you possibly can without singeing it.

Seams made between strips of polyester lace ribbon and two grids cut from garden fleece, with synthetic knitting yarns fused over them.

Method
1. Place two pieces of nylon organza, one on top of the other, on the glass. Cut out a row of motifs and put them to one side (see page 18 for cutting shapes using templates).
2. Place another piece of nylon organza on the glass and arrange a horizontal row of motifs just below the top edge, leaving 2cm (¾ in) gaps between motifs.
3. Press the narrow edge of the ruler just below the top edge of the motifs and make a tiny horizontal running-stitch mark on each one, to fuse them to the backing. You need to make a tiny running-stitch mark, as just making a little dot mark will not fuse them. Cover the work with another piece of nylon organza, aligning the top edge with the top edge of the backing fabric.
4. Place the ruler horizontally, just below the running-stitch marks made on the motifs, and slowly run the tip of the soldering iron at quite an upright angle along the edge, cutting right through to the glass to fuse all the layers together. Leave the ruler in position and remove the excess strip of fabric.
5. Open out the fabrics; the motifs will be neatly sealed within the seam.

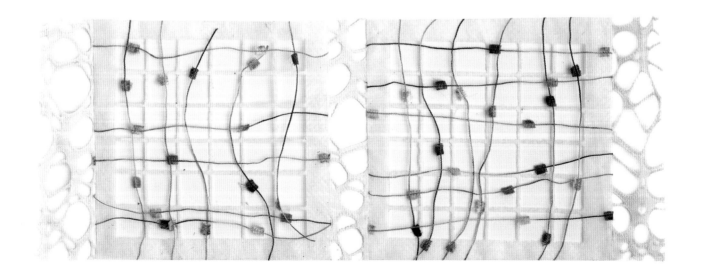

This small sampler shows motifs and loops fused between seams and embellished with hand stitching.

Cutting ribbons from fabric

Ribbons can be used in a variety of ways, but in this instance they will be used for the lacing and looping methods, which bring a pretty three-dimensional quality to a piece of work. I suggest you use nylon organza before experimenting with other lightweight fabrics.

Requirements
- Basic tools and equipment
- Two pieces of nylon organza, each about 15cm (6in) square, in contrasting colours

Method
1. Place the pieces of organza, one on top of the other, on the glass.
2. Place the ruler horizontally on the fabrics, about 1cm (½in) down from the top edge, and run the tip of the soldering iron slowly along, making absolutely sure that you are cutting right through to the glass. If the cut edge isn't perfectly straight, try running the tip at a slightly more upright angle along the ruler, and always run it in the same direction.
3. Move the ruler down the fabric and cut again, this time about 6mm (¼in) below the previous line, and repeat this down the length of the fabrics. If the ribbons stick to the glass, try not to disturb them until you have cut the last one, as this greatly helps you to control the fabric and prevent the edges from puckering or distorting. Carefully lift them off the glass when you have finished.

Fusing a row of loops between a seam

Method
1. Cut a number of ribbons, as described above, making each 6mm (¼in) wide, and then cut them into 6cm (2½in) lengths and put them to one side.
2. Place a piece of nylon organza, for the backing fabric, on the glass.
3. To make a loop, fold a ribbon in half so that the ends meet and hold them together on the backing fabric, with two ends about 1cm (½in) above the top edge and the folded edge lying on the fabric.
4. Place the edge of the ruler on the loop, about 3mm (⅛in) below the edge of the backing fabric. Make a short running-stitch mark in the centre to fuse it down. Repeat this process, fusing evenly spaced loops across the width of the fabric.
5. Cover with another piece of organza, aligning the top edge with the top edge of the backing fabric.

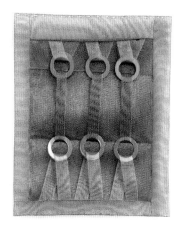

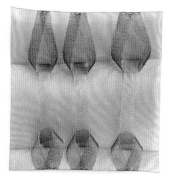

6. Tilt and press the narrow edge of the ruler very firmly, just below the running-stitch marks on the loops. Run the tip of the soldering iron slowly along the edge, holding it at a very upright angle, and then remove the waste strip.

7. Open out the fabrics; the row of loops will be securely fused between the seam.

Fusing loops between seams. Sequin washers are slipped onto the ribbons before making the loop.

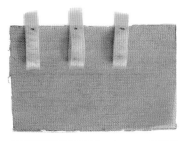

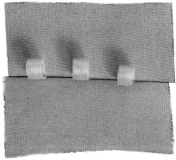

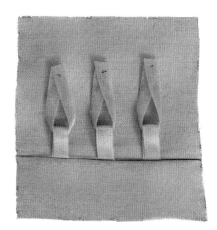

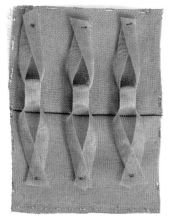

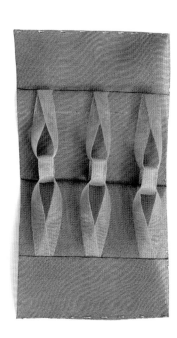

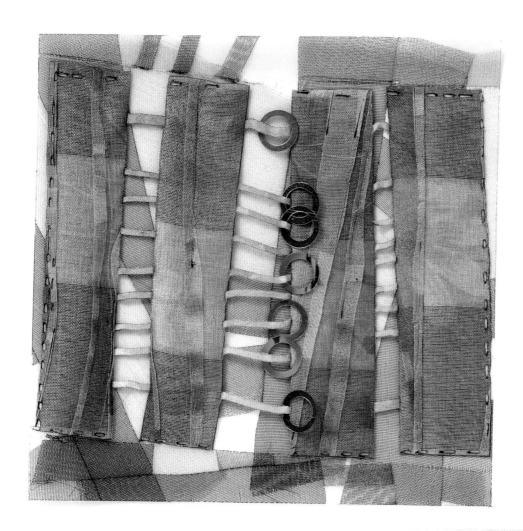

Shapes were cut from several layers of polyester fabric, using a metal washer as a template. Ribbons cut from one layer of polyester on top of nylon organza were threaded through the shapes and fused, using the looping method, to a backing of layered fabrics.

Narrow ribbons with sequin washers threaded onto them were fused to the edge of wider strips, then fused to a backing of patchworked pieces.

Loops within loops

The method described above can be decorative in itself, but the technique can be carried further by looping another loop on each side of every loop.

Requirements
- Basic tools and equipment
- Several 6cm (2½ in) ribbons, of a contrasting colour to the ones you made on pages 52–53

Method
1. First fuse a row of loops of one colour between fabrics, following the method described previously.
2. Pass a 6cm (2½ in) length of contrasting colour of ribbon through the first loop. Align the ends to form a loop and fuse them above the seam to the backing with a short running-stitch mark, made 3mm (⅛ in) from the ends. Try not to pull the loops too tightly as this will distort the seam.
3. Cover the work with another piece of organza, aligning the top edge with the ends of the second set of loops.
4. Repeat steps 6 and 7 in the previous method.
5. Turn the work upside down and repeat step 2.
6. Cover the work with another piece of organza, aligning the top edge with the ends of the third set of loops.
7. Repeat steps 6 and 7 in the method on page 53.
8. Place the work on a backing of nylon organza and then run the tip of the soldering iron along the edge of the ruler around all four sides, to cut the work to size. This strengthens and flattens the work.

Further suggestion
Try using commercially made synthetic ribbons.

Two seams were made with loops fused between them, a second ribbon was slipped through them to form another loop and a small circular motif was stitched over the ends. Finally, another narrow ribbon was laced through the first set of loops.

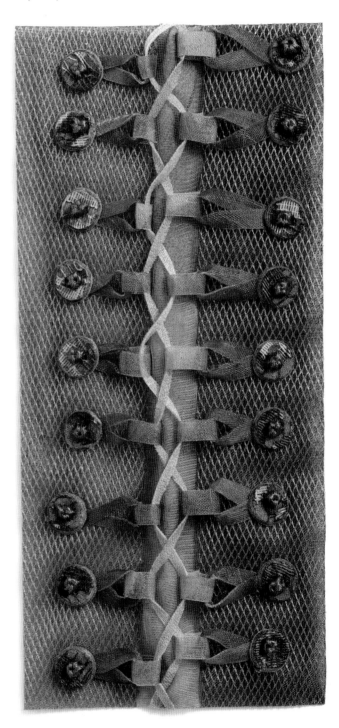

Ribbons and metal stencils

You can use the strips shown here to make a small panel by arranging them on a backing fabric and adding some motifs and shapes. Alternatively, you could fuse the strips to a backing fabric and then cut out motifs or shapes.

Requirements

- Basic tools and equipment
- Nylon organza
- Patterned polyester fabric
- Metal stencils

Method

1. Place two pieces of nylon organza on the glass, with a piece of polyester fabric on top, aligning the top edges.
2. Place the ruler horizontally on the fabrics, about 1cm (½in) below the top, and run the tip of the soldering iron along the edge to score a row of running-stitch marks, basting them together.
3. Slide the ruler about 1cm (½in) down from the marks and run the tip of the soldering iron slowly along, making sure that you cut right through to the glass.
4. Place the stencil so that the shape you are going to cut out sits about 6mm (¼in) below the previously cut line; cut out a row of evenly spaced shapes, and leave them in position on the glass.
5. Position the ruler about 6mm (¼in) below the shapes and cut across with the soldering iron. Cut another row of shapes, using the same stencil. Place the ruler 1cm (½in) below them and cut across again.
6. Place a different colour fabric on the work, just below the last cut line. Place the ruler just below the edge of the new fabric and run the tip of the soldering iron along the edge, cutting right through to the glass.
7. Change the stencil; cut out another row of shapes, and then repeat step 5. Always leave the cut-out shapes and strips stuck to the glass.
8. The strips will become thicker the more often you add another top fabric. However, if you don't want really thick strips, but you do want to introduce another colour, it is possible to carefully peel the last layer off the fused edge before adding another fabric.
9. When you have finished all the cutting, carefully lift the strips off the glass, trying not to disturb the motifs. If the motifs are firmly stuck to the glass, you can leave them in place for use in the following method.

Layered strips and cut-out shapes.

Fusing motifs attached to the glass on strips

An added bonus, after cutting out motifs, is that sometimes they remain attached to the glass. If this happens, instead of lifting them off, it is possible to fuse them directly onto another piece of fabric or onto a strip.

Method

1. Cover the motifs with one or two layers of nylon organza; you need to be able to see or feel them through the organza.

2. Tilt and press the narrow edge of the ruler firmly on the organza, so that it sits across the centre of the motifs. Rest the tip of the soldering iron against it and make a very short running-stitch mark on the centre of each motif. Make the mark as lightly as possible, so that it will hardly be seen from the front, and then leave everything in position on the glass.

3. Place the ruler on the work 1 or 2cm (approximately ½ in), first above and then below the motifs, and run the tip of the soldering iron along to cut off the excess fabric. If you have several rows of motifs, repeat steps 2 and 3 down the length of the fabric.

4. Gently slip the edge of the ruler under the strips to ease them off the glass with the motifs fused to them.

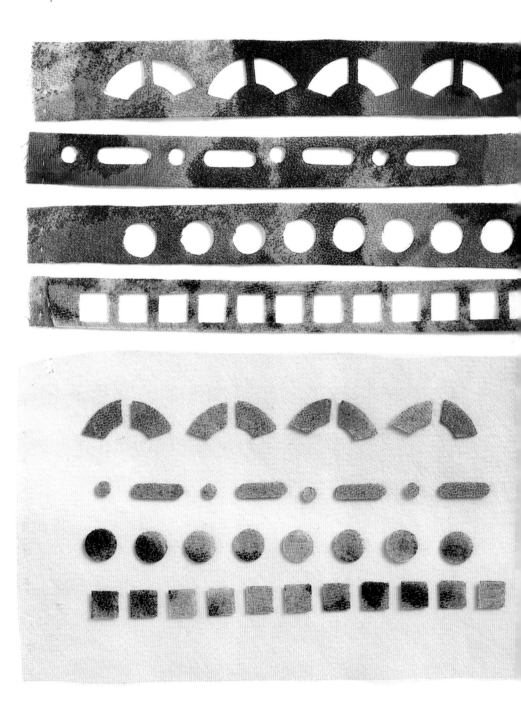

Using stencils to cut shapes in ribbons and then fusing the remaining shapes onto another fabric.

Strips, stripes and patterns samplers

For this sampler, choose colours that go well together and remember that you might have to back any awkward fabrics with nylon organza.

Requirements

- Basic tools and equipment
- A variety of polyester fabrics, patterned and plain
- A piece of relatively firm polyester fabric (I have used a black polyester lining fabric) on top of one piece of nylon organza, large enough to arrange the strips one below the other, leaving a border of at least 3 to 4cm (1¼ to 1½ in) around all four sides.
- A piece of mountboard larger than the backing fabric
- One piece of acrylic felt for the backing

Preparation

Using some of the methods described so far, select straight rulers, fancy-edged rulers, stencils and templates and use them to cut a number of strips and motifs in co-ordinating colours.

Make up the strips by fusing some of the narrow strips to wider ones and fusing motifs to others until you have an interesting assortment.

Spend some time planning the order in which the strips will be arranged and fused to the backing fabric. When you are happy with the layout, place them carefully to one side, in the chosen order.

Tip

Using mountboard instead of glass has two advantages: firstly, when you fuse your fabrics together, they will grip to the fibres of the board and secondly, if your glass isn't large enough, mountboard makes a useful temporary substitute. The board does, however, become full of score marks; this would hinder the smooth running of the soldering iron, so you cannot use it for long.

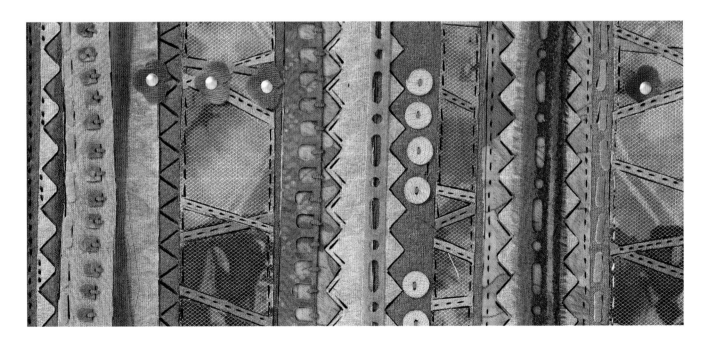

Close-up area of the sampler shown in full on page 60.

Layered strips and shapes fused to a backing fabric and finished with simple hand stitching.

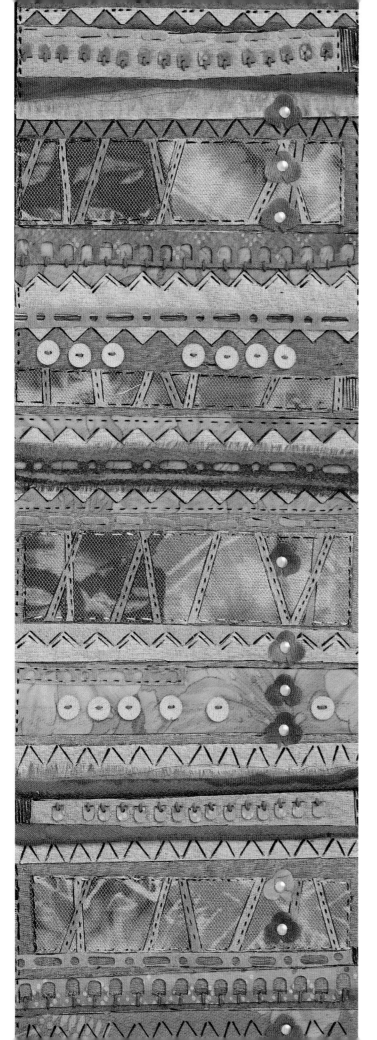

Method

1. Place the polyester lining fabric on top of the nylon organza on the mountboard.

2. Fuse the two layers to the mountboard with a row of running-stitch marks, made across the width of the fabrics, 1cm (½ in) down from the top edge.

3. Starting 3cm (1¼ in) below the running-stitch marks, fuse the strips one by one in the chosen order to the backing fabric by making two small running-stitch marks at both ends of every one of the strips, going right through to the mountboard. The strips can easily be lifted off if you want to reposition them.

4. While everything is on the mountboard, measure and mark the work to the finished size by making a few running-stitch marks around the border (viewfinders are very useful for helping you to determine the size). Align the edge of the ruler on the marks and run the tip of the soldering iron slowly along to cut off the excess fabric on all four sides, and then lift the sampler off the mountboard.

5. Fuse the sampler to the acrylic felt with a border of running-stitch marks.

6. It isn't really necessary to fuse the top and bottom of all the strips to the backing, because you can add some stitching at step 7, but you could fuse some of them with some running-stitch marks. This would add definition to the sampler (remember that the deeper you score, the darker the mark will be).

7. At this stage, you could add some decorative hand stitching and a few extra small motifs. I have attached some with a small decorative metallic brad.

Strips, Stripes and Pattern sampler.

Very rigid batons

I have used these batons in quite a few of the techniques in this book. The idea for making them came to me after using dried-out leaf stems in my altered book project. If the tip of your soldering iron is very sharp and fine, it is possible to cut extremely neat batons, as narrow as two or three millimetres (less than an eighth of an inch), and as straight as the edge of the ruler.

For very stiff, rigid batons, you need up to six or seven or maybe more layers, depending on the thickness of your fabrics, interleaving them with nylon organza. The nylon organza may not always be necessary, but if the fabrics you use are flimsy and soft, the nylon organza certainly helps.

Requirements

- Basic tools and equipment
- Depending on the thickness and how rigid you want the batons to be, use six or seven layers of non-stretch medium-weight fabric
- Nylon organza, to interleave between the layers

You should choose interesting fabrics for the top and bottom layers, but for the layers between you could use up cheap plain fabrics, while bearing in mind that the cut edge of the fused layers will be seen. If you use dark colours, the fused edges will appear almost black.

Important point

Always remember to test the fabrics to make sure they are all entirely synthetic by cutting a slit with the tip of the soldering iron across both the warp and the weft.

Method

1. Starting and finishing with an interesting fabric, layer the fabrics on the glass, placing one on top of the other and interleaving the nylon organza between them.
2. Place the ruler horizontally on the fabrics, about 2cm (¾in) down from the top. With the tip of the soldering iron, score a row of running-stitch marks along the edge to fuse the layers together.
3. Starting about 1cm (½in) below the marks and 3 to 4cm (1¼ to 1½in) in from the edge of the fabric, run the tip of the soldering iron at a very upright angle slowly along the ruler for however long you want the batons to be, leaving 3 to 4cm (1¼ to 1½in) uncut to the right. Be very sure you are cutting right through to the glass; if you think you need to make the cut again, always run the tip in the same direction. This process takes a while if you have lots of layers to cut through.
4. Depending how wide you want the batons to be, move the ruler down the fabrics and cut again (I usually cut them about 2 to 3mm or less than ⅛in wide).
5. Continue cutting evenly spaced batons down the length of the fabric. You must try not to disturb the batons and clean the tip of the soldering iron regularly on the wire wool, as this makes it easier to cut consecutive strips and also prevents distortion.
6. Trim the batons to length in one go, using sharp scissors. If they are very rigid, the ends should be very neat, but if there are a few wispy bits, just run the tip of the soldering iron across to neaten them.

Further suggestion

To cut the batons to length using the soldering iron, place the edge of the ruler about 1cm (½in) in from the ends and run the tip slowly from top to bottom. If the batons are stuck together at the ends, just snap them apart. Alternatively, if they are firmly attached at the ends, it might be possible to manipulate them to form spokes or other shapes.

Fusing batons together to form a circle of spokes

1. Using the method described previously, many rows of batons were cut, the first and last cuts being longer than the rest. The batons were then cut to length at one end only; at the other end, the cut was made 3mm (⅛ in) away from the ends in the form of a fringe or a comb.
2. The fringe was wrapped around a pencil and the edges were tightly butted and fused together where they met. The fusing, which was a little tricky to accomplish, was done by stroking the tip of the soldering iron three or four times across and beyond where they met, so that a film of melted fabric spread across the join.
3. While the batons were still around the pencil, they were carefully splayed out to form the spokes and gently flattened as far as they would go without bending them. They were then gently slipped off the pencil.
4. The batons were arranged on a backing of Vilene, which had been printed with a photocopied image. A piece of mirror (shisha) glass was placed under the centre of some, while others had a circular motif or upright spokes fused in the centre of them.
5. The spokes, motifs and mirrors were held in place either with small fusing marks or with a stitch passing between the spokes and into the backing fabric (see page 44 for a close-up).

The batons form the shape of a comb before the two ends are fused together.

The spokes were manipulated and the ends were fused together to form complete circular flower shapes then stitched to a backing of printed Vilene.

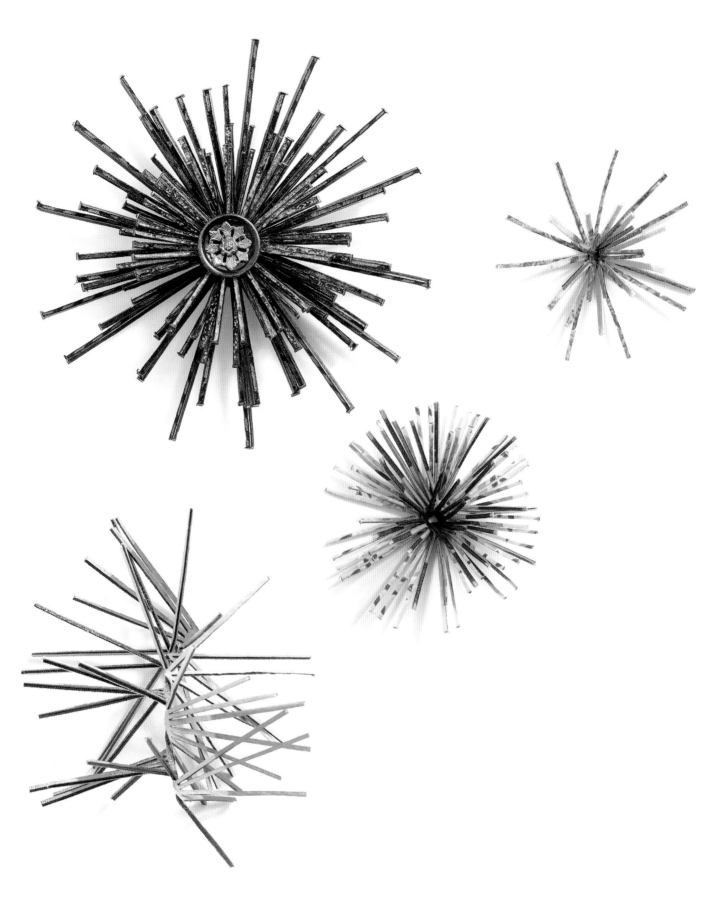

Layered and manipulated spokes.

Altered book

I was set a project to make a piece of work by altering a book. I bought an old French phrase book with faded brown pages for 50p. Some may think that it is sacrilege to cut into a book, but I recently heard someone on the radio saying that thousands of paperbacks have been used to make the foundations of some motorways, which got me thinking that maybe it's not such a bad idea to use an old book to make a piece of artwork.

I experimented first with two other small books bought from a charity shop, using a sharp scalpel to score lines into the pages, after which I tried to weave them together. The weaving didn't work, but after scoring lines through lots of pages in one go, ideas began to take shape and the method described opposite evolved.

After cutting through the pages, the stems were pushed down into the slit as far as they would go and a letter of the alphabet was popped on the end of each one.

The stages involved

1. I drew a large circle around a template in the centre of the third page, which was on the right-hand side of the phrase book. Next, I used a very sharp scalpel, held against the edge of a metal ruler, to score evenly spaced vertical lines from top to bottom over the whole of the circle, cutting through as many pages as possible.

2. The cut edges of the scored lines gripped all those pages together, so I was able to turn them all over in one go. I then drew another circle, of the same size, in the centre of the following page. Again, I scored vertical lines through as many pages as possible, cutting just about halfway through the phrase book.

3. Starting from the first cut page, I scored a line horizontally across the centre of the vertical strips, cutting through as many pages as possible, and then continued until all the vertical slits were cut across the centre.

4. From the back of the last cut page, I pushed all the strips through to the front of the first cut page. The strips all fanned out within and around the edge of the circle, like a chrysanthemum, leaving just a small slit in the centre.

5. In my 'might come in useful' box, I had a bundle of dried, very rigid, twig-like brown leaf stems, which I pushed down into the slit as far as they would go.

6. Using alphabet-shaped metal templates, I cut the letters out of Vilene (Pellon) that had been stained with tea, covered with one piece of light brown nylon organza.

7. I supported the remaining pages of the phrase book with card to form a box shape and coloured it to blend in with the edges of the pages. This made a firm base on which to fuse the word 'Catchphrase'

8. Lastly, I popped a letter of the alphabet on the end of every stem, so that they looked as if they were all bursting out of the phrase book. It was a fun piece of work to do.

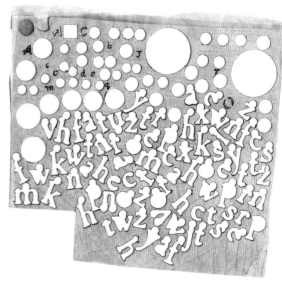

The negative shapes left after cutting out the letters for the Altered Book.

The letters bursting out from the centre of the book.

3 MARK-MAKING

In this chapter I have combined many of the methods covered so far in the book, and have used a variety of fabrics and depths of fabric to create different types of marks and textures.

Two contrasting-coloured fabrics on a base of five plain fabrics. Shapes were cut out of the top layer first, then all the layers were fused together with marks and pattern.

Using rulers and templates on multiple layers of fabric, this sampler incorporates many techniques, including mark-making, light and heavyweight motifs, batons, ribbons and beads.

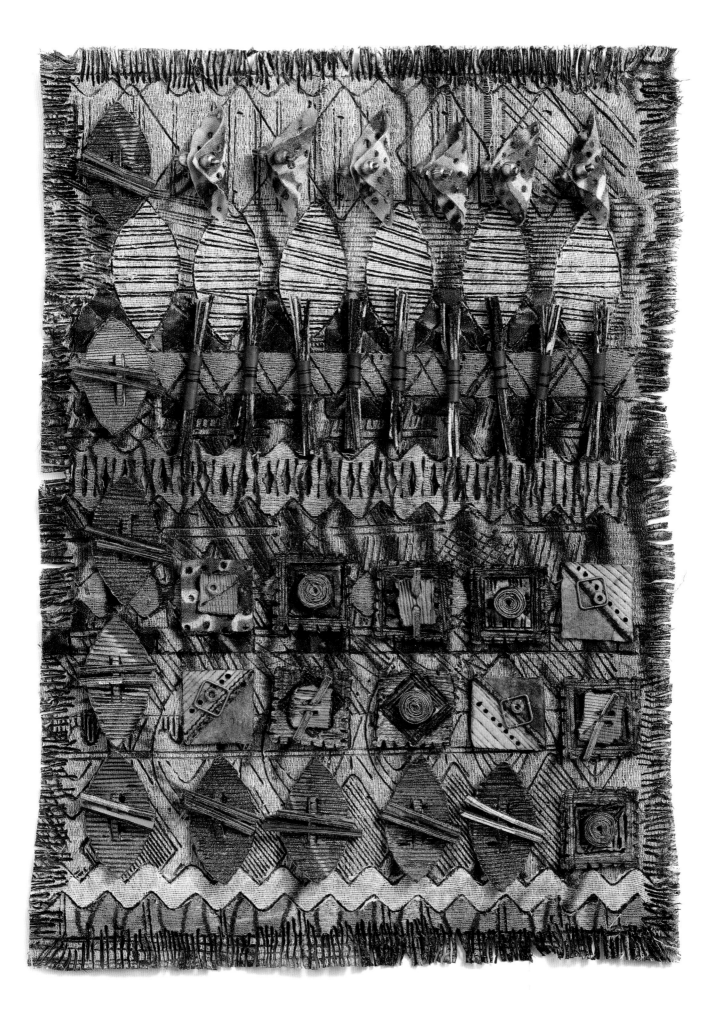

Using rulers and templates on multiple layers of fabric

Use inexpensive light- to medium-weight, non-stretch polyester fabrics, such as polyester scarves, dressmaking fabrics, linings, curtain fabrics or charity-shop finds. Most of these do not have to be interesting, because they won't be seen, but choose an interesting one for the top and bottom layers, if these will be seen.

It is important to put pressure on the ruler or template as you make marks on layered fabrics, because this eliminates a lot of the air between layers, helping to make the fabric much firmer and the marks neat and sharp.

This sampler incorporates the following:
- A backing of layered fabrics, fused together with pattern and mark-making techniques.
- Lightweight motifs and strips fused to the backing with fine scored lines.
- Heavyweight motifs with crinkly, curled-up edges, scored with fine lines and with batons pushed through slits made in the centre of the motifs.
- Bundles of batons pushed through rubber tubing.
- Strips rolled up to form beads.
- Square motifs, folded and held together with batons and beads.
- A fringed border, cut freehand through all the layers.

Requirements
- Basic tools and equipment
- For the base, four or five layers of fabric, plus a few layers of nylon organza
- Three or four pieces of patterned or plain lightweight polyester fabrics
- Simple geometric templates to fit between lines (see step 4, right)
- Straight-edged ruler
- Fancy-edged rulers

Method
1. Layer the base fabrics on the glass, placing one on top of the other, with the nylon organza interleaved between layers, finishing with an interesting fabric on top.
2. Press the narrow edge of the ruler firmly about 1cm (½in) down from the top and run the tip of the soldering iron along to score a straight line across the top of the work. The tip should score deep into the layers, but not right through to the glass, and you should be able to see a very positive dark line. If you score right through to the glass too easily, add a couple of extra layers to the base.
3. Move the ruler 2 to 5cm (1 to 2in) down and score another line. Continue scoring lines this distance apart until the layers are fused together down the length of the fabric.
4. Place a template between the lines and score a strong mark all around the edge. Move the template to the right; score a whole row, and then fill in the shapes with scored lines or patterns, made either along the edge of the ruler or around a template. Change the template and score in between other lines until you have filled the whole fabric with pattern. Then put the work to one side.
5. Using patterned and plain fabrics and a range of templates and rulers, cut a number of lightweight shapes and strips from one or two layers of fabric.
6. Put the base back on the glass and arrange the shapes and strips on top of it. One by one, put the template you used to cut out each shape back on top of it, in exactly the same position, and score a strong mark all around the edge with the tip of the soldering iron to fuse it flat to the backing. Next, score fine lines or decorative patterns over the shapes, using the edge of the same template or the edge of the ruler.

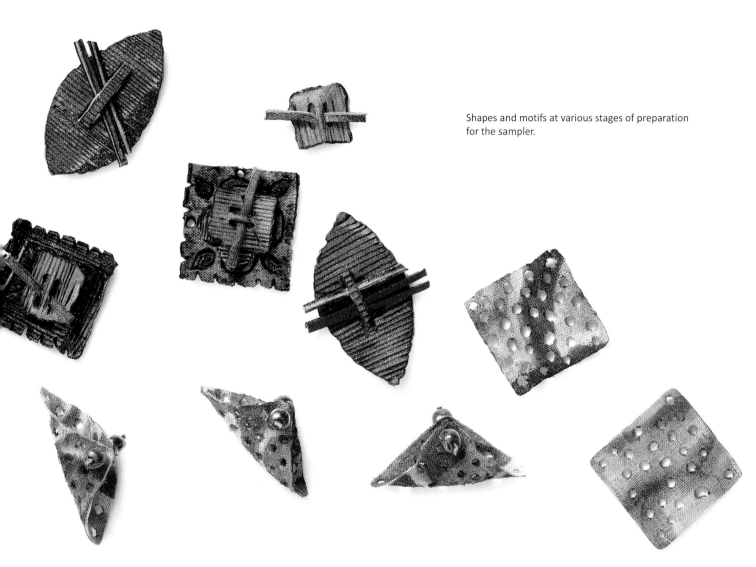

Shapes and motifs at various stages of preparation for the sampler.

7. Place the ruler on the very edge of the strips and score a strong line along the edge with the tip of the soldering iron to fuse them to the backing.

8. Score extra lines and pattern in other areas to build up the surface texture.

9. To make some strong heavyweight motifs or shapes, place six or seven layers of fabric on the glass, again with an interesting one on top, and score fine lines along the edge of the ruler, one below the other, cutting deep into the layers. Place a template on top and cut all around the edge, cutting right through to the glass, and then stitch or fuse them in place on the sampler.

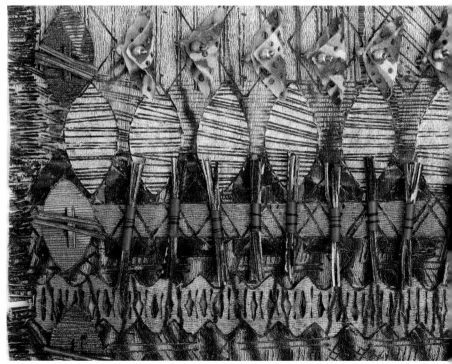

Close-up area of the main sampler.

Freehand mark-making

If you make marks lightly on multiple layers of fabric without using the pressure of a ruler or a template to compress the layers, there will be a certain amount of air between the layers. As result, the marks will not be neat and sharp; instead, they will be more like slits, and the layers beneath will show through.

Requirements
- Basic tools and equipment
- For the base, four or five pieces of lining fabric or fabric of a similar weight
- Two or three pieces of interesting lightweight polyester fabric, all the same size

Reminder
Remember to clean the tip of the soldering iron on the wire wool now and again as you work.

Method
1. Layer the fabrics on the glass, one on top of the other, finishing with interesting ones for the last two or three layers.
2. Tilt and press the ruler about 1cm (½ in) in from the edge of the fabrics and score a border of short running-stitch marks around all four sides, just to fuse the layers together.
3. With the tip of the soldering iron at an upright angle, lightly score patterns and marks freehand into the topmost layer; the marks will look like slits and the layer beneath with show through them.

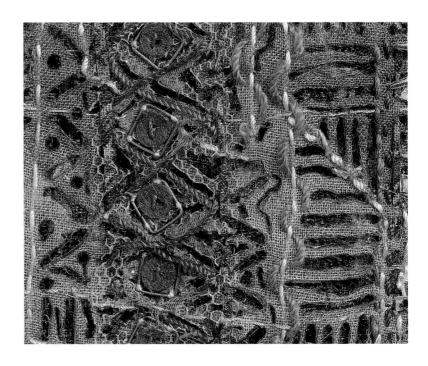

Close-up of the marks made freehand on multiple layers of fabric.

Freehand mark-making on multiple layers of fabric, with a few strips of polyester net added for extra texture; this was embellished with beads, motifs, strips cut from layered fabrics and simple hand-embroidery stitching. Background: block-printed brown paper with a black fusible web and pressed leaves ironed over it.

Making marks raised and stiffened with the heat tool

For this technique, you need to use a heat tool. If this is new to you, make sure you read the manufacturer's safety precautions first. Always point the heated end of the heat tool away from you, as it gets extremely hot and will burn you or singe your clothes if you are careless.

Requirements
- Basic tools and equipment
- One piece of black polyester lining fabric and one piece of Evolon, both the same size
- Drawing pins (the three-pronged thumbtacks used to prepare silk for painting are easier to push into wood than the usual drawing pins)
- Wooden frame
- Heat tool

Method
1. Place the black lining fabric on the glass with the Evolon on top.
2. Being careful not to completely cut out any areas and holding the tip of the soldering iron very upright, doodle squiggles and patterns freehand, but firmly, over the fabrics, being sure you are cutting right through to the glass so that the lines stick to it.
3. Remove the work from the glass then stretch and pin it quite tightly on a wooden frame with the drawing pins.
4. With the back of the work facing you, lean the frame upright against something, ensuring that there is a lot of space around it so that nothing behind it will be damaged by the heat tool.
5. Hover the end of the heat tool about 4 to 6cm (1½ to 2½ in) away from the work and slowly work your way over it; the black lining fabric will melt in areas where you stay a little longer with the tool, leaving just the Evolon. The squiggles and marks will stretch apart and will be stiffened by the heat. The loose ends of shapes will become distorted and forced through to the front and the back of the work. Hold the tool a little nearer and stay slightly longer over areas where you want the shapes to be even more raised, but be careful not to create unwanted large holes by staying too long or too close in any one area.

Mark-making on Evolon, raised and stiffened with the heat tool.

Mark-making on Evolon, raised and stiffened with the heat tool: draw the basic shapes within a template on the Evolon first and use them as a guide for making the marks, and then fill in the spaces with freehand squiggles and marks.

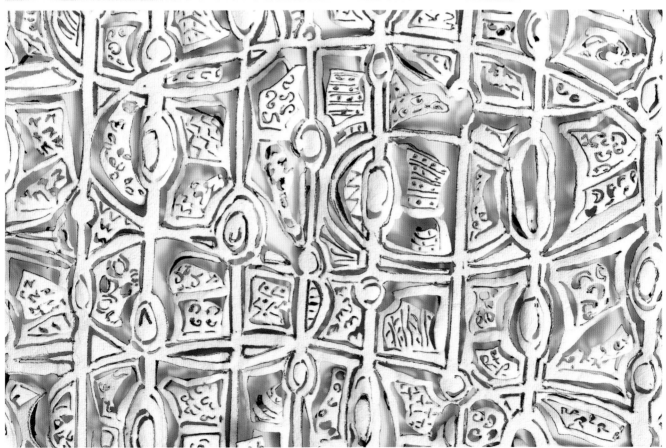

Marking a design on fabrics with running-stitch marks

The running-stitch mark is not only very useful for basting or fusing layers together; it can also be used to mark a design and fuse the layers together at the same time. The marks can be quite strong and decorative, if scored deeply into the layers.

This technique is a very useful way of marking a design on fabric that is difficult to draw on or is too opaque to allow a design to be traced onto it. It reminds me of the old traditional method known as 'pricking and pouncing'. I used a pencil to draw around the border and the shapes within a plastic template to mark the design on paper nylon fabric. Plastic templates or masks are available in numerous designs and can be bought from most craft shops or from traders at craft and stitching shows, but you could, of course, draw your own design. The paper nylon is removed after the marks have been made. Alternatively, you could also try another smooth-surfaced fabric, such as white polyester lining fabric, but you need to be able to see your design through it.

Requirements

- Basic tools and equipment
- One plastic template or mask for the main design
- One piece of paper nylon (this is a crisp, white, semi-transparent fabric about the thickness of tracing paper)
- For the base, six pieces of medium-weight fabric, such as polyester or acetate lining fabrics (any plain fabrics will do, because they will not be seen)
- One interesting colourful lightweight patterned fabric (I have used a polyester patterned scarf)
- One piece of white Sizoflor
- One small tapestry needle (not a sharp-pointed needle)
- One large circular metal template or any other simple geometric shape

Method

1. Place the plastic template on the paper nylon and use a pencil to draw around the border and the patterns within it.
2. Layer the base fabrics on the glass, one on top of the other, and then add the decorative piece, followed by the Sizoflor.
3. Place the paper nylon with the design traced on it on top of the Sizoflor.
4. Starting somewhere near the centre, place the ruler (the mirror plate) on the line of the design and make short running-stitch marks along the edge, passing through the paper nylon and into the layers beneath (a tiny dot mark won't make a good mark nor fuse the layers together properly; it has to be a very short running-stitch mark).
5. Continue working your way from the centre to the outer areas until the design is fully marked out.
6. Now for the tricky part – removing the paper nylon to reveal the design. You do this with a careful tearing action, using your fingers to help to keep the layers beneath from lifting. With practice, it is possible to tear it off quickly.
7. The running-stitch marks should now be clearly visible on the white Sizoflor and the layers beneath should be fused together.
8. Join up the running-stitch marks by drawing into them freehand with the tip of the soldering iron, making a continuous scored outline around the design (it's like doing a dot-to-dot puzzle).

The design was traced onto paper nylon and running-stitch marks were scored through it into the fabrics beneath, then the nylon paper was removed.

9. To lift the Sizoflor off the positive areas of the design (leaving it in place in the background negative areas), slip the tip of the tapestry needle just underneath the Sizoflor, as close as possible to the inside edge of the scored line. Push the tip right up against the line; gently lift it to break the seal, and then work your way around all the areas to be lifted off. Use your fingers to stop the background Sizoflor from lifting.

10. You may end up with a few whiskers of Sizoflor. These can easily be removed with a quick touch of the tip of the soldering iron.

11. Now, working from the centre outwards, fill the background (the negative areas) with a flowing rhythmic pattern of running-stitch marks, which will also stabilize the whole piece. To do this, place the metal template on the work; score short running-stitch marks all around the edge, and then fill in the shapes with more marks. Use the edge of the same template to fill in the remaining background areas with more rhythmic, flowing running-stitch marks.

The running-stitch marks used to mark out this design on layered fabrics were inspired by the rhythmic running stitches used in Kantha quilting.

Removing selected layers of fabric

For this technique, the design is first marked onto layers of fabric, after which chosen areas of the top layer are removed to reveal the layer beneath.

Requirements

- Basic tools and equipment
- For the base, three pieces of medium-weight fabric, such as acetate lining fabric
- Two pieces of polyester fabric – one should be multicoloured; the other will be the top layer and should also be interesting and contrasting in colour

Method

1. Layer all the fabrics on the glass, the polyester fabric on top of the base fabrics, and baste them all together with a row of running-stitch marks, made horizontally along the edge of the ruler made about 1cm (½in) down from the top.
2. Slide the ruler about 3cm (1¼in) down the fabric and score a line deep into the layers, but not right through to the glass, to mark the top edge of the outer border of your design. Slide the ruler down and score again.
3. Being careful to keep the layers flat on the glass so that there is no air between layers, score lines vertically, horizontally and diagonally, until you have scored a design composed of rectangles, squares and triangles.
4. To remove selected areas of fabric from the top layer and reveal the layer beneath, insert the tip of a tapestry needle just underneath the surface and push it as close as possible to the scored line.
5. The needle prevents the layers beneath from being touched by the soldering iron, and will also protect your fingers. Run the very tip of the soldering iron along with the needle, as close as possible to the line, all around the edge of the fabric to be removed. Once you have a big enough flap of fabric to hold with your fingers you won't need to use the needle, except at very tight corners.
6. When you have finished removing the top layer from all the selected areas, score a second line as close as possible to the edge of each of the lines to neaten any rough edges and to emphasize the design, adding extra lines where you think they are needed.

Further suggestion

You can use the same technique to remove selected areas of fabric after a design has been stitched, rather than scored. First stitch the design on the layered fabrics and then use the method described above, using your stitching line as your guide. The stitching is going to come into contact with the soldering iron, so you must use a thread, such as cotton, silk or a strong rayon, that doesn't melt.

It's always best to test the threads before you start stitching. To do this, hold the thread under tension on the glass and run the tip of the soldering iron over it several times; if it melts, don't use it.

Scoring a design on layered fabrics and then removing
selected areas from the top layer.

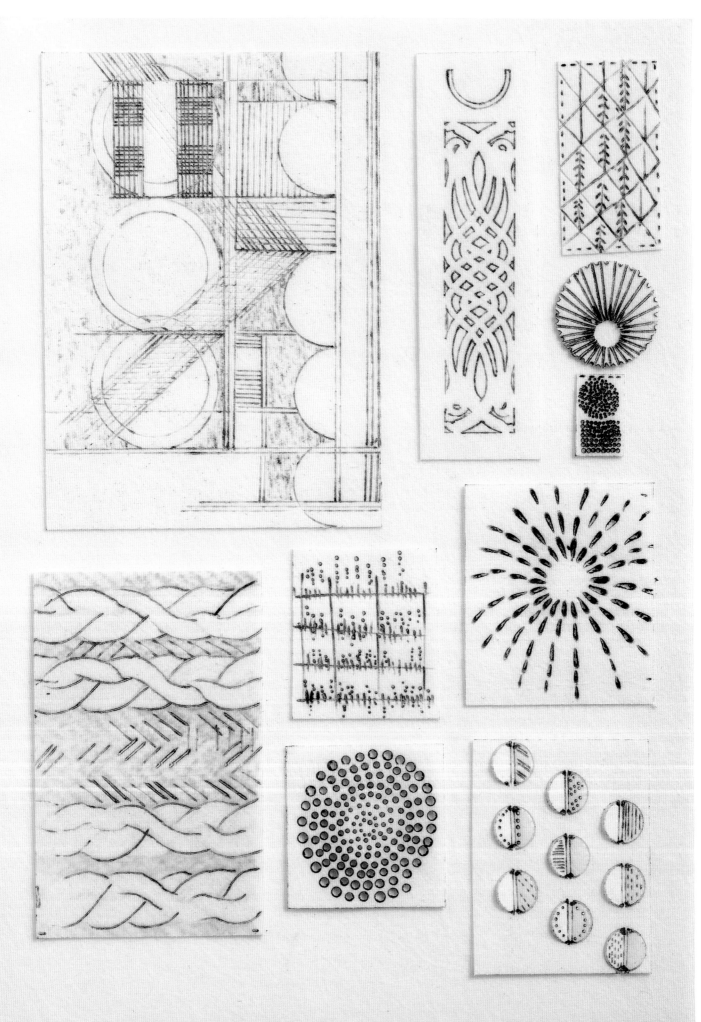

Vilene samplers 1 and 2: Mark-making

Two samplers show the effects of mark-making on Vilene.

Sampler 1

A variety of singe marks were made using the following methods:

- Run the tip of the soldering iron at a shallow angle quickly and lightly along the edge of a ruler, either around the edge of a template or freehand, to make very pale brown marks.
- Run the tip at a shallow angle and much more slowly to make strong brown marks. Hold the tip for longer and at a more upright angle for deeper marks, but be careful not to score right through to the glass.
- Stroke the surface Vilene with the tip at a shallow angle, using a back-and-forth motion, to make light, textured marks.
- Score lightly halfway through a motif in order to bend and raise it.
- Run the tip around a stencil.
- Make tiny eyelets by holding the Vilene off the glass and gently and slowly pushing the tip vertically through, then slowly withdrawing it.
- Make droplet-shaped eyelets by first putting the very tip on the Vilene then lowering it at a shallow angle. The lower the tip, the longer the droplet will be.

Sampler 2

This sampler shows mark-making and cutting motifs, using templates:

- Small circular holes and tiny eyelets, linked with cross stitches.
- Square apertures with a lace stitch filling.
- Square motifs held down with lazy daisy stitches.
- Small raised circles, not entirely cut out.
- Small circles squeezed into slits.
- Tiny holes or eyelets.
- Concentric rings cut with washers.
- Twisted border (see method described on page 80).
- Circles fused into cone shapes with slits and dark crinkly edges (see method described on page 81).

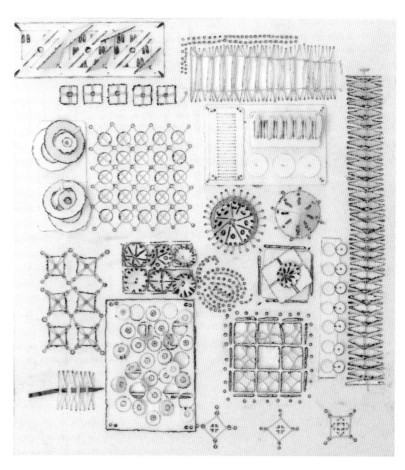

Left: Vilene sampler 1: singe marks on Vilene.
Right: Vilene sampler 2: singe marks and motifs on Vilene.

Twisted border

Sampler 2 shows a technique inspired by the twisted borders seen in drawn-thread work, where a number of threads within the warp or weft of a fabric are withdrawn and the remaining threads are twisted together by running thread through them to form a decorative pattern or border.

Pinning the Vilene (Pellon) to a frame raises it off the glass, which makes the edges of the slits very rough, dark brown and textured because a wider area of the tip is in contact with the fabric. I quite like the rough, dark edges, because they give a good contrast to the white Vilene, but if you prefer a cleaner edge, you should work with the Vilene flat on the glass, and remember to clean the tip more often.

Requirements

- Basic tools and equipment
- Vilene (Pellon)
- Wooden frame
- Drawing pins to pin the Vilene to the frame
- Needle and thread

Method

1. Pin the Vilene to the frame and place the ruler horizontally on top. Rest the tip of the soldering iron on the edge; push it right through the fabric, and run it along the edge of the ruler so that it makes a straight slit, about 3cm (1¼ in) in length. Make an even number of parallel slits, one beneath the other, about 3mm (⅛ in) apart, to form the bars. Be careful not to make the bars too narrow, as they could break when you twist them.
2. Thread a needle with a strong thread. Secure it to the Vilene on the back of the work, about 6mm (¼ in) above the centre of the first bar, and bring it through to the front of the work.
3. To make a simple twist, pass the needle over the first two bars and then slip it back under the second bar and over the first bar. Pull the thread back under the first two bars and repeat the process over the next two bars. Finish off with a couple of holding stitches on the back of the work.

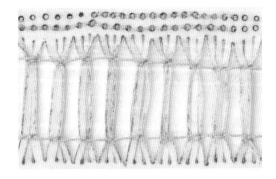
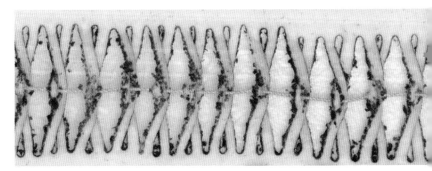

Vilene cone shapes

Circular templates can be used to make cones, as shown here.

Requirements
- Basic tools and equipment
- Vilene (Pellon)
- Small metal circular template

Method
1. Place the Vilene on the glass and run the tip of the soldering iron around the template to cut out a number of circles.
2. Make a cut from the very centre to the outer edge of a circle by running the soldering iron along the edge of the ruler.
3. Overlap the cut edges to form a cone shape.
4. Holding the shape tightly, score short marks across the overlapped edges with the tip of the soldering iron to fuse it down, while taking care not to burn your fingers.
5. Make two tiny holes in the bottom centre of the cone with the tip of the soldering iron. These will be used to stitch the cones to the sampler.
6. Slowly run the tip of the soldering iron around the rim to make a singed crinkly dark edge, which also helps to fuse the overlapped edges together.
7. Make a few decorative slits or tiny holes around the sides of the cone with the tip of the soldering iron.

Opposite page: twisted borders from Sampler 2.
Below: Vilene cone shapes from Sampler 2.

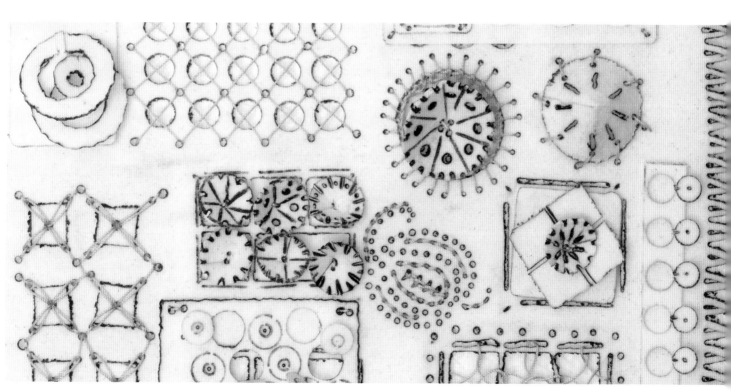

Vilene sampler 3: Mirror work

Traditional mirror work, as seen in Indian embroidery, is combined with decorative stitching. The result is very bright and colourful. Small round mirrors are held down on the fabric with four long stitches. Buttonhole stitch is then worked over them to form a border, which also holds the mirror in place.

My sampler is very neutral in colour, but you could, of course, use coloured threads and dye or print on the Vilene first. Vilene is quite rigid and cuts easily with the soldering iron, but you must remember to keep cleaning the tip if you want the cut edges to be clean and neat.

The sampler shows the following elements:
- Holding the mirror glass in place with four long stitches, with buttonhole stitch worked over them.
- Buttonholed Vilene rings stitched in place through tiny eyelets.
- Vilene rings embellished with singe marks and eyelets.

The four basic steps for holding the mirrors in place on a backing of Vilene are shown at the bottom of the sampler, and the method is described right.

Requirements
- Basic tools and equipment
- A fine cotton perlé thread or similar
- Vilene (Pellon)
- Mirror glass (also known as shisha glass)

Method
1. Secure the thread to the back of the Vilene with a couple of small stitches and place the mirror glass on top.
2. Bring the needle out at the top right, as close as possible to the edge of the mirror glass, and make one long vertical holding stitch over it and through to the back of the Vilene.
3. Bring the needle out at the top left of the glass and make another long holding stitch over it and through to the back.
4. Make two horizontal holding stitches in the same way, passing the thread under and over the two vertical stitches, and finish off on the back of the Vilene with a couple of stitches.
5. Work buttonhole stitch over the holding stitches, not too tightly, and then work a second row through each of the buttonhole loops. Take the thread to the back of the work and finish off with a couple of stitches. At this stage, don't worry if you can see the edge of the mirror glass, because the final stage will stretch the loops over it.
6. With the tip of the soldering iron, make a ring of evenly spaced tiny eyelets into the Vilene, just a little way from the edge of the buttonhole loops.
7. Secure a new thread to the back of the Vilene and bring it to the front through one of the eyelets; pass it over the buttonhole loop opposite to it and then back down through the same eyelet and up through the next eyelet. Repeat this all around the border. When you have completed the circle, finish off with a couple of stitches on the back of the work.

This mirror-work sampler shows the basic technique and the development of ideas, using eyelets, buttonholed Vilene rings, rows of buttonhole stitch around the inner edge of a cut-out circle, and the use of buttons, sequins and Vilene rings, embellished with singe marks.

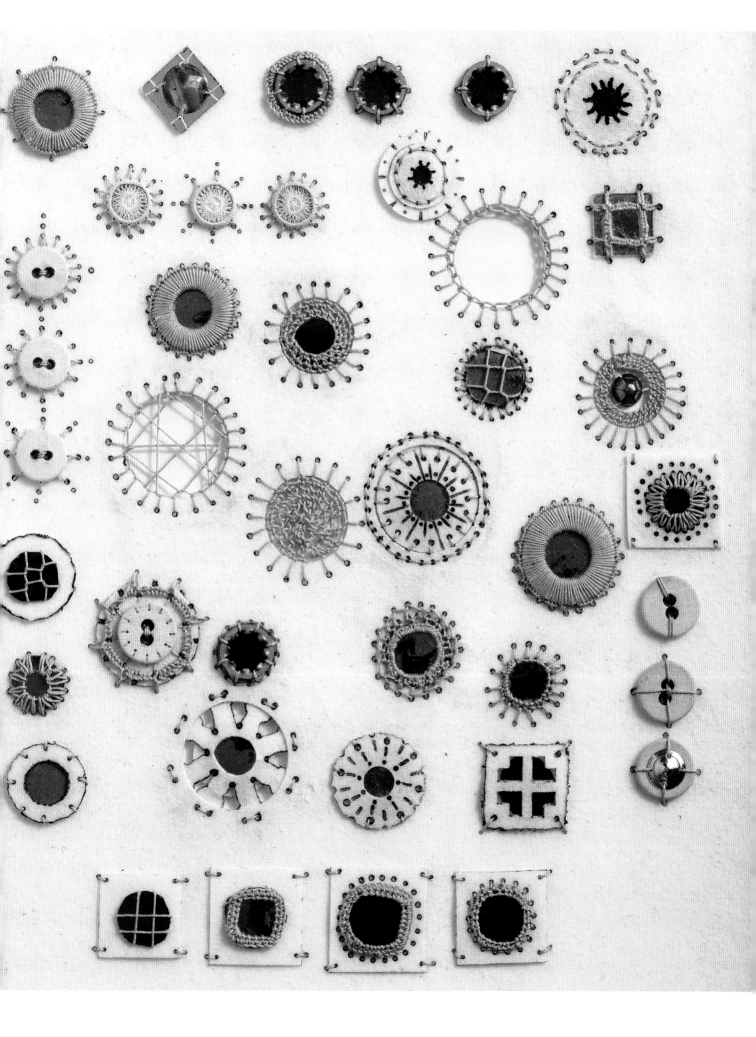

Book cover

The book cover was made by first soaking an ivory-coloured piece of acrylic felt for several hours in a mixture of 250ml (roughly ½ pint) PVA to 1 litre (2 pints) of water, to stiffen it. After this, it was rolled in an old towel to soak up the excess liquid, left flat to dry, brushed with two coats of cheap quality gesso, and left to dry again.

The soldering iron was used to score running-stitch marks and patterns into it. Tiny eyelet holes were made and a few simple shapes were cut out freehand and fused to other areas.

Using a needle and thread instead of the soldering iron, running stitch was worked in and around the marks with various weights of black thread. The cover was lined with calico and a machine-wrapped cord was hand-stitched around the border.

The four buttons were cut from several layers of polyester fabric with a piece of gesso-painted felt for the top layer. They were attached to the ends of two machine-wrapped cords, long enough to wrap twice around the cover.

Book filled with trial samples of mark-making on Vilene.

Acrylic felt was soaked in PVA and water to stiffen it, and when dry it was coated with gesso. Marks were scored into it and small shapes were cut out and fused to other areas; it was then embellished with hand stitching.

This is based on tapa textiles and uses motifs cut
from tea-stained Vilene. The little square pockets,
crossed batons and square beads were made from
layered fabrics.

Tapa textiles

The inspiration for the colours and patterns in this piece (and other pieces in this book) were taken from *Traditional Tapa Textiles of the Pacific*, by Roger Neich and Mick Pendergrast, a beautiful book which describes the history, manufacture and decorating of cloth made from the bark of certain trees. The piece shown here is made up of three layers and uses many of the techniques described in this book.

Layer 1
A piece of woven silk with patterns and colours reflecting those found in tapa textiles.

Layer 2
A piece of Mexican amate bark paper found in my stash of goodies

Layer 3
The third layer was assembled in the following order:

1. Small square button shapes cut from layered fabrics, with a bead and two short batons at the centre of each one, were stitched in position on the bark paper.
2. Large circles, cut from tea-stained Vilene, were scored with radiating singe marks and a cut was made from the middle to the outer edge of each one. They were slipped around and under the small square button shapes.
3. An eyelet was made on all four corners of little square pockets (see page 98), and the ends of two very stiff crossed batons were pushed through them to support the shape.
4. The pockets were stitched between the rows of circles.
5. Small wooden beads were stitched to the background bark cloth.

4 MANIPULATING SHAPES & MOTIFS

In this chapter I have used the cutting and fusing technique and a variety of fabrics to create three-dimensional surfaces using just a very basic square template or a metal grid.

Using a metal grid as a template, squares were cut out from layered fabrics, but one corner of each square was left uncut so that it was still attached to the grid. The four corners were then folded and fused to stand upright around a small square base.

Creating three-dimensional surfaces

Take a simple shape, such as a square, score some slits into it and then manipulate it to form a three-dimensional surface.

Requirements

- Basic tools and equipment
- Two pieces of very lightweight polyester fabric in contrasting colours or patterns and one piece of nylon organza, all of which should be the same size and large enough for you to cut a number of squares from them
- A 3cm (1¼in) square metal template
- A circular template or coin and a washer – one that will sit in the centre of the square leaving a border of at least 4mm (⅙in) all around

Reminders

- For neat, straight edges, run the tip of the soldering iron in one continuous movement along the edge of the ruler.
- As you cut the slits, the fabric sticks to the glass; this really helps to keep everything under control, so where possible leave everything in position on the glass and move on to the next step.

Method 1

1. Place a piece of polyester fabric right side down on the glass and cover it with the nylon organza. Place the second polyester fabric right side up on top of it.
2. Baste all the layers together, about 2cm (¾in) down from the top edge, with a row of running-stitch marks, made by running the tip of the soldering iron along the edge of the ruler.
3. Starting at the top left of your fabric, about 1cm (½in) below the marks, run the tip of the soldering iron around the edge of the square template. Cut right through to the glass, but leave the bottom left and the top right-hand corners uncut so that the square is still attached at these two corners.
4. Leave a gap of about 3mm (⅛in) and cut the next square, leaving the bottom right and top left corners uncut.
5. Reversing the sequence of the cut corners, cut two more squares about 3mm (⅛in) below the first two.
6. Run the tip of the soldering iron at an upright angle along the edge of the ruler to cut evenly spaced parallel horizontal slits from the top to the bottom of the squares, but make the first and last slit shorter than the rest. It is important not to cut the slits too close to the sides of the square.
7. On each square, bring the two cut corners together, overlap them and slip a pencil underneath. Press the tip of your fingernail firmly over the corners to hold them tightly together and make a very tiny running-stitch mark on the overlapped corners to fuse them together. Try to avoid touching the slits as you do this.
8. Repeat the process in every square.
9. Fuse the finished piece to backing fabric of a contrasting colour.

Manipulated squares showing the uncut corners and the slits.

The finished piece is fused to a backing
of two layers of polyester organza.

Method 2

1. Follow steps 1 to 5 in method 1.
2. Place a coin in the centre of the square; run the tip of the soldering iron around the edge, but leave a tiny uncut area opposite the two uncut corners of the square, so that the circle is still attached at these two points.
3. Score parallel lines on the circle or in the area surrounding it, as you wish.
4. Fuse the two cut corners as in step 7 in method 1.

Another variation

1. Follow steps 1 to 5 in method 1.
2. Using a washer instead of a coin, place it in the centre of the square; run the tip of the soldering iron around the outer edge, but leave one tiny part uncut so that the circle can be repositioned at step 5, below.
3. Next, cut around the centre of the washer and leave everything in place on the glass.
4. Run the tip of the soldering iron at an upright angle along the edge of the ruler to cut evenly spaced parallel slits in the area surrounding the circle, and then lift the small circle from the centre.
5. Flip the circle over so that the reverse side of the fabric is showing; reposition it and with a quick touch of the tip of the soldering iron fuse one tiny area of the edge of it to the edge of the square aperture.

Further suggestions

At step 3 of method 1, leave only one corner of a square uncut, which allows it to be flipped over and seen from the reverse side. The cut corner is then fused in position with a quick and tiny touch of the tip of the soldering iron.

Manipulated squares showing the variations given in method 1, plus some further variations.

When making a sampler, ask yourself 'what if I fused it this way or that way, or folded it in half and made a seam across the centre of it?' – let the 'what if' factor kick in. Background fabric is a photocopy printed on Lutradur.

Manipulating squares to form a three-dimensional shape

Here, two squares are fused together back to back to form a 3-D diamond. The fabric must be strong enough to withstand stretching the slits at step 4 without tearing.

Requirements

- Basic tools and equipment
- One piece of polyester lining fabric
- Two lengths of polyester brocade ribbon
- A 3cm (1¼ in) square metal template

This diagram shows the position of the slits in step 2.

The squares before and after being manipulated.

Method

1. Sandwich the polyester fabric between the two brocade ribbons and cut out two squares.
2. Place a square on the glass in a diamond shape, right side up. Cut evenly spaced horizontal slits from just below the top corner to just above the bottom corner, but leave a wider gap between them at the halfway point. Do the same with the other square. It is important not to cut the slits too close to the sides of the square.
3. Make a row of tiny eyelets with the tip of the soldering iron across the halfway point of each square.
4. Being careful not to tear the fabric, very gently stretch the slits and manipulate the corners and the sides of the squares so that the slits widen out and the shape becomes slightly domed.
5. With the slits facing you horizontally, place the squares on top of each other, right sides together, in a diamond shape and fuse the top and bottom corners together with a short running-stitch mark.
6. Overlap the two unfused corners of one of the squares and slip a pencil underneath. Press the tip of your fingernail firmly over the corners to hold them tightly together and make a very tiny running-stitch mark on the overlapped corners to fuse them together. Try to avoid touching the slits as you do this. Then fuse the two unfused corners of the other square in the same way.

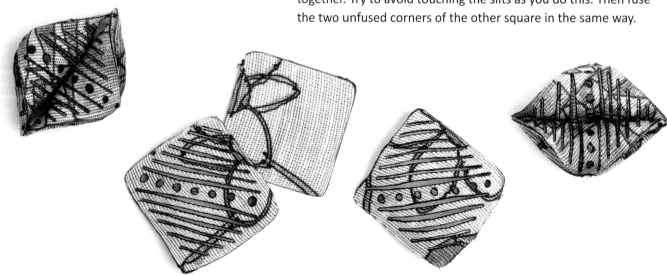

Two squares were fused together back to back forming a three-dimensional diamond shape. A backing of Evolon was lightly coloured with acrylic paints, then scored with marks and spirals, and the shapes were fused onto it. A grid cut from Evolon on a base of black polyester lining fabric was laid over the shapes and fused to the backing with running-stitch marks.

Manipulating a square by fusing the corners together to form a three-dimensional shape.

Manipulating shapes and motifs

Chain links: manipulating square-shaped motifs

Squares can be manipulated to form three-dimensional shapes that could be linked together in long lengths or used for jewellery.

Requirements

- Basic tools and equipment
- One piece of nylon organza, the same size as the other fabrics
- Two pieces of quite firm but lightweight polyester fabric in contrasting colours (I have used a polyester metallic fabric also known as polyester metallic tissue)
- A 5cm (2in) square metal template (you could try using other sizes)
- A circular metal template or a coin large enough to cut one circle out of each quarter of the square, leaving a small border around each
- A tiny circular metal stencil

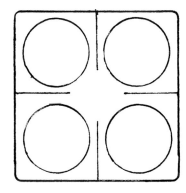

Chain links showing the position of the cuts and the circular apertures

Further suggestion

At stage 5, lift the bottom corner; slip the aperture over the top corner, and then give the points a little tug.

Method

1. Put the nylon organza on the glass between the two pieces of polyester metallic tissue.
2. Place the square template on top and run the tip of the soldering iron around the edge to cut out several squares. If they stick to the glass, leave them in position, as it will help with the next stage.
3. At the midpoint of each side, run the tip of the soldering iron along the edge of the ruler to make a 1cm (½in) cut in towards the centre. Cut the rest of the squares in the same way.
4. Place the circular template on a square and cut out four evenly spaced circles, one from each quarter, leaving a small border around each one. Repeat with the rest of the squares and then lift everything off the glass, putting the circles to one side for use in other projects.
5. Place one of the squares on the glass so that it faces you in the form of a diamond shape. Lift and align the bottom corner with the top corner, laying them flat on the glass, and lightly fuse them together with a very tiny mark just a little way in from the edge. Positioning the tiny circular stencil over the mark, run the tip of the soldering iron around the edge to fuse the corners permanently together and then remove the tiny circle.
6. Fold back the two remaining corners of the square so that the points are aligned and fuse them together in the same way.

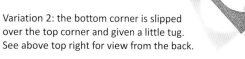

Variation 1: only the top and bottom corners are fused together; make two and fuse them back to back at the two remaining corners.

Variation 2: the bottom corner is slipped over the top corner and given a little tug. See above top right for view from the back.

Little pockets

Squares can also be manipulated to form small pockets.

Requirements

- Basic tools and equipment
- Three pieces of lightweight non-stretch, patterned polyester fabric
- Two pieces of nylon organza
- A 3cm (1¼ in) square metal template

Method

1. Layer the fabrics on the glass, starting and finishing with a patterned fabric.
2. Place the template on top and run the tip of the soldering iron around the edge. Cut out several squares then put them to one side.
3. Make two thick rigid batons (see page 61) for each square.
4. Hold a square off the glass and push the tip of the soldering iron a tiny way in to make a small hole, about 3mm (⅛in) in from each corner. The hole should be small enough for a baton to be pushed through and held in place with little or no slack.
5. Place a pair of batons, one on top of the other in the form of a cross, and fuse or stitch them together where they cross.
6. Bring the corners of the square towards the centre to form a pocket and push the ends of the crossed batons through the corner holes so that the cross sits firmly in place and holds the sides of the pocket upright.

See also Tapa textiles, page 87.

Manipulating squares to make little pockets with crossed batons. After step 2 a small circular gold motif was fused to the centre, and at step 6 the batons were fixed together with a small metallic brad.

Manipulating squares and slits to form a hollow ogee shape

These squares with slits cut into them have to be strong enough to stand being stretched without tearing, so you have to be careful not to cut the slits too close to the sides and corners of the squares. I used Evolon on top of nylon organza.

Requirements
- Basic tools and equipment
- Two pieces of nylon organza
- One piece of Evolon
- 2.5cm (1in) square template

Development stages for the hollow ogee shapes.

Method

1. Place the two pieces of organza on the glass with the Evolon on top and fuse all the layers together with a row of short horizontal running-stitch marks, about 1cm (½in) down from the top edge.
2. Place the template on the fabric and run the tip of the soldering iron around the edge. Cut out two squares.
3. Place a square facing you on the glass in the form of a diamond. Position the ruler on top and run the tip of the soldering iron along the edge to cut horizontal parallel slits right through to the glass, 3mm (⅛in) apart, from top to bottom. If the slits are made too close to the sides or the corners they will break when you stretch them at the next stage. Repeat the process with the other square.
4. Very gently stretch the slits and the sides of the squares so that the slits widen out and the shape becomes slightly domed, but be careful not to tear the fabric.
5. With the slits facing you horizontally, place the two shapes down on the glass side by side, right sides up. Overlap the two corners where they meet (see diagram on page 101) and fuse them together with a short running-stitch mark, made parallel to the slits. Next, bring the shapes together, wrong side to wrong side; overlap the opposite two corners and fuse them together. When you do this, you will need to slip something metal, such as a coin, underneath the corners.
6. Place the shape on the glass with the slits facing you horizontally and fuse the top two corners together, then the bottom two corners, with a tiny running-stitch mark parallel to the slits.
7. With the shape off the glass and the slits facing you horizontally, hold the left- and right-hand corners and squash them together so that they meet precisely at the centre to form the ogee shape. At this stage, the shape holds its hollow form quite well, but you could gently tease and stretch the edges and the slits to refine the shape – try not to crease them. Then stitch or fuse them to a backing fabric, as in the photograph shown on page 101.

Large hollow ogee shapes made with block-printed Evolon backed with nylon organza. A needle and thread was passed through the centre of the shape and out through the back. It was not pulled tight, so the shape retained its hollow form. A small bead was slipped on the needle and the thread was passed back through the hollow and out to the front, where another bead was added and stitched in place.

Small hollow ogee shapes fused to square-shaped motifs within a grid.

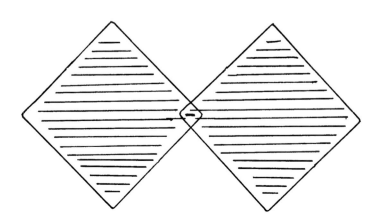

Step 5: when overlapping the corners, fuse the squares together with a short running-stitch mark.

Manipulating squares within a grid: Method 1

Four corners are folded and fused to stand upright on the grid around a little square base. For my main sample I used a grid of ten by twelve squares, but for the methods described below you will just be working on two over two squares to make a trial sample. Methods 1 and 2 look interesting from both sides of the work before they are fused to the backing fabric, so give some thought to the colours of the fabrics you use.

Requirements
- Basic tools and equipment
- One piece of Sizoflor for a backing fabric – this is quite rigid, which helps in supporting the upright areas, but you could experiment with other fabrics
- One piece of polyester lining or similar fabric
- One colourful polyester fabric
- A metal grid – this type of grid is sold in quite large sheets at DIY shops or garden centres; the squares within it measure 2 x 2cm (¾ x ¾ in)

1. Layer the fabrics on the glass, one on top of the other: first the Sizoflor, then the lining fabric, and then the colourful one.
2. Press the grid firmly on the fabrics and run the tip of the soldering iron along the inside edge of four squares, stopping about 3mm (⅛ in) before you reach the centre cross point of the grid.
3. Starting with the bottom left-hand square, lift this corner and fold it flat over the centre cross point of the bars onto the top right-hand square, taking it just as far as it will go without stretching it. Press the narrow edge of the ruler very firmly about 2mm (¹⁄₁₂ in) away from the fold and fuse it down with a very short running-stitch mark. Press it flat into its original place and repeat with the three remaining squares.
4. The folds and fusing marks form a small square base around which the four squares stand upright. Adjust, overlap and tweak the squares so that they interlink and stand upright around the base.
5. Back the work onto fabric of a suitably contrasting colour.

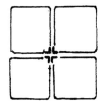

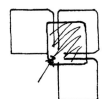

Manipulating squares within a grid, showing the bars, the cuts and the folds.

Manipulating squares within a grid method 1. The four corners are folded and fused to stand upright on the grid around a little square base. The finished piece is fused to a mosaic of nylon organza shapes, fused to Vilene.

Manipulating squares within a grid method 2. Working on a grid of six by seven squares, I varied the direction in which I have cut along the bars as well as the number of folds and the direction in which they are folded over. At step 4, I also cut out tiny squares in some of the triangular shapes instead of cutting out one large square.

Manipulating squares within a grid: Method 2

In this alternative method, four corners are folded towards the centre of the grid and fused down with a small running-stitch mark. Again, you will just be working on two over two squares to make a trial sample.

Requirements

- Basic tools and equipment
- One piece of polyester lining fabric or something similar
- One piece of nylon organza
- One piece of polyester fabric, patterned or plain, in a toning or contrasting colour to the lining fabric
- Metal grid (2cm x 2cm)

1. Layer the lining fabric, the organza and the patterned fabric in that order on the glass.
2. Hold the grid firmly on the fabrics, run the tip of the soldering iron along the inside edge of the bars to make the cuts shown in Diagram 1, and then turn the work over.
3. Lift and fold the corners in towards the centre and fuse them down with a very tiny running-stitch mark – see Diagram 2.
4. Position one square of the grid so that it sits in the centre and run the tip of the soldering iron around the inner edge of all four bars to cut out a square – see Diagram 3.
5. Choose which way up you want the sample to be and back it onto a suitably contrasting-coloured fabric. See 4 and 5 below.

Diagram 1
Cutting along the bars.

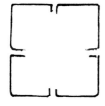

Diagram 2
Fold and fuse the corners.

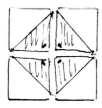

Diagram 3
Cut out a square shape in the centre.

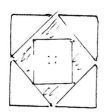

Sample showing steps 1–5, plus some variations.

Manipulating squares within a grid: Method 3

The techniques described in method 2 can be developed to create raised and padded areas. Once again, you will be working on two over two squares to make a trial sample.

Requirements

See list for Method 2, page 105.
In addition, cut some circles from Kunin felt; the size should be large enough to sit centrally over four squares (two over two) leaving a 3 to 4mm (⅛ to ⅙ in) border all around. Kunin felt is a very soft acrylic felt.

1. At step 3, Method 2, before you fold and fuse the four corners down on the back of the work, place a circle of felt in the centre of the square and then turn the work back over to the front (see diagram below).

2. Place a smaller circular template in the centre of the padded area; press very firmly to compress the layers, and run the tip of the soldering iron around the edge to cut the circle.

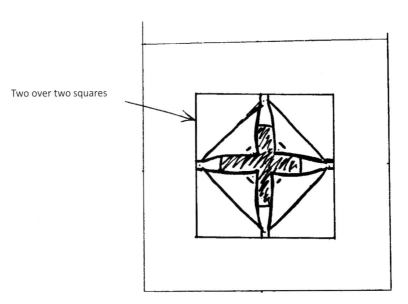

Two over two squares

On the back of the work, before you cut and fold the four corners down, place a circle of felt in the centre.

Manipulating squares within a grid method 3, showing raised and padded areas. This sample shows four over four squares.

Little kite shapes

Depending on which corners you fuse together, it is possible to make many variations
of these small shapes.

Requirements

- Basic tools and equipment
- Two quite crisp and firm, but not thick, polyester fabrics in similar or contrasting colours
- A 4½ cm (1¾ in) square metal template (alternatively, just use the ruler)
- One tiny circular template

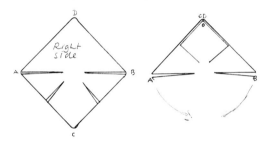

This diagram shows where to make the cuts for the kite shapes.

Method

1. Place one fabric right side down on the glass with the other piece right side up on top of it. Place the metal template on top and cut out a number of squares.
2. With the square facing you in the form of a diamond, make a 2.5cm (1in) long cut from the left- and right-hand corners, points A & B on the diagram, in towards the centre.
3. Halfway between points A/C and points B /C, make 1.5cm (⅝ in) cuts in towards the centre.
4. Lift the bottom corner C to align and lie flat on the top corner D and fuse them together with a tiny running-stitch mark, just in from the corners. Place the circular stencil over the mark; run the tip around the edge of it, and remove the little circle.
5. Bring points A and B down so that they meet with wrong sides together and fuse them together in the same way.

Little kite shape samples.

Background fabric – a marbling technique was used on a piece of Lutradur; this was very kindly prepared for me by Craig Joubert (see page 117).

Manipulating shapes and motifs

Take a triangle

For the first method here, I used lightweight Lutradur, which makes the shape quite rigid. By contrast, for the second one I used a lightweight polyester fabric, which gives a soft edge to the folds of the shape.

Requirements
- Basic tools and equipment
- 9cm (3½ in) square of Lutradur (30)

Take a triangle, make a cone shape and manipulate it.

Method 1
1. Cut the square of Lutradur in half across the diagonal with the soldering iron to make two triangles.
2. Fold a triangle in half, but don't crease it, and fuse the longest sides together by running the tip of the soldering iron along the ruler just a little way in from the edge of the fabric right through to the glass, then remove the little excess strip.
3. Fold the open end of the cone back on itself until the tip of the cone sits within about 2cm (¾ in) from the bottom of the shape.
4. Fold the open end of the cone back on itself again until the shape holds itself upright and will sit flat on its base.

Method 2
1. Take a 10cm (4in) square of lightweight polyester fabric and fold it in half across the diagonal.
2. Fold it in half again and fuse the two sides together then remove the excess strip.
3. Follow on from step 3, above; after step 4, bring the open end back on itself again.

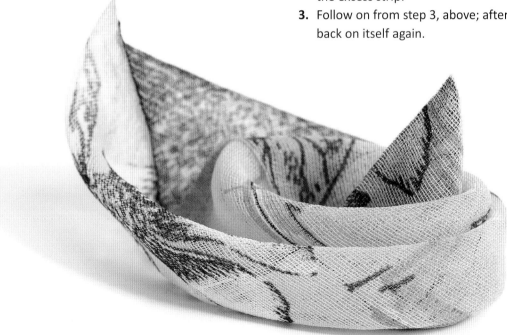

5 COLOUR AND PATTERN

Wherever I have used a plain white fabric, such as Vilene, Lutradur or Evolon, as backing fabric or for cutting out shapes and motifs, I have used some of the following quick and easy ways for adding colour, pattern or texture to them.

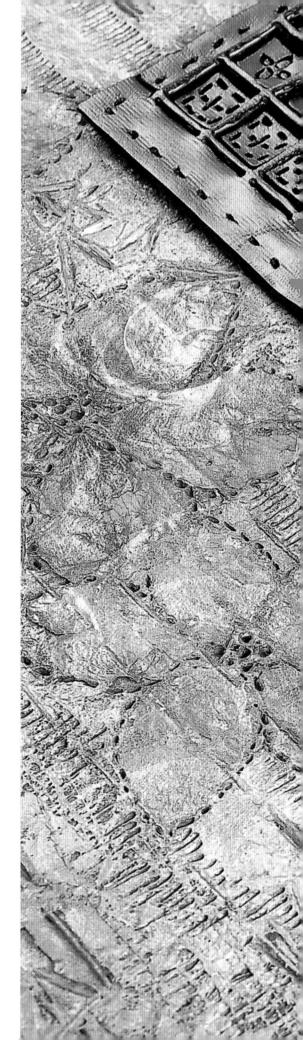

Background: acrylic felt was soaked in a mixture of PVA and water and, when dry, painted with gesso. Using a heavy cotton thread, long stitches were stitched into it, then the whole piece was given another coating of gesso. Pressed flower petals backed with Bondaweb (Wonder Under) were then ironed onto the background, and the whole piece was given two coats of acrylic wax and dried with a hairdryer. Using the soldering iron, strong running-stitch marks were scored around the edge of the petals and into the rest of the background. Foreground: gold PVC fabric backed with nylon organza was placed on top of a metal grid backed with black acrylic felt. Lines were scored along both sides of the bars within the grid right through to the felt, and decorative marks were scored deep into the little squares.

Cutting slits to raise and manipulate a surface

I chose this particular design because I knew the elongated diamond shapes and the straight lines within it would be ideal for this technique. The image is copyright-free and was taken from *Visual Elements 3 – Marks and Patterns Clip Art*, published by Columbus Books.

Making the design

To make this design, I placed a piece of Evolon on top of a piece of polyester lining fabric on the centre of a piece of photocopy paper. I then ran the tip of the soldering iron along the edge of the ruler to score a row of running-stitch marks along the top edge of the fabrics, to fuse them to the paper.

I then taped all four sides of the fabrics securely to the paper with masking tape, making sure that the tape and fabrics lay perfectly flat, leaving no untidy edges which might jam the photocopier. I ran the fabric through the photocopier and then carefully removed the fabrics from the paper, but left the masking tape on the fabric.

With the image right side up, I taped the fabric on the glass, making sure it was neatly stretched and that there were no bumps or wrinkles anywhere. Running the tip of the soldering iron along the edge of the ruler, I scored long slits on the lines within the design.

I took the masking tape off the fabric and stretched the slits apart to form a slightly raised surface. Next, with the slits stretched under tension, I fused all four sides of the fabric to a backing of acrylic felt, using running-stitch marks. I then added a few stitches with a needle and thread, just to make sure that the slits remained stretched and in place.

To finish, I cut two slits, one below the other, in the centre of each of the small Vilene circles. I then threaded them onto the long strips cut from layered fabrics and wove them randomly in and out of the slits.

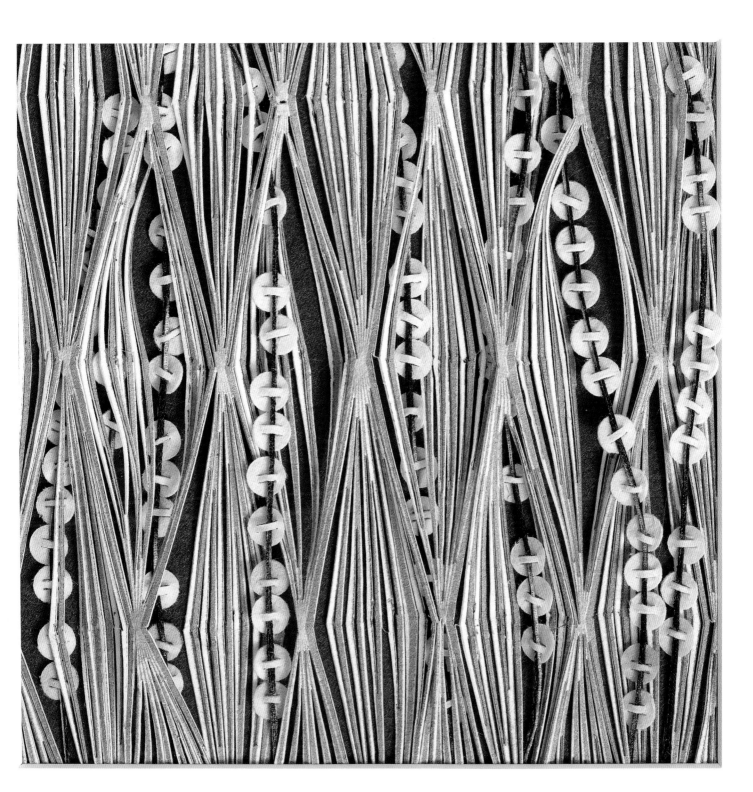

Cutting slits into a design to raise and manipulate the surface.

Photocopying onto fabric

You can use an inkjet printer to photocopy either your own design or a copyright-free image onto a variety of fabrics. The colours may not be as strong as those of the original, but subtle effects can be produced for use as backgrounds or for cutting out motifs and shapes.

You have to be happy about putting fabrics through your printer. If you are worried about damaging your printer, it might be a good idea to buy a cheap photocopier to use just for this purpose. I have experimented with Vilene (Pellon), Evolon and Lutradur and other lightweight polyester fabrics.

Photocopy printed onto Vilene. Slits were cut into the Vilene and circular motifs were slotted into the slits.

Method

Cut the fabric smaller than A4 and tape it to a piece of photocopy paper with masking tape, making sure that the tape is well within the edge of the paper and there are no frayed edges peeping out or any wrinkles or creases anywhere that might cause the printer to jam. When you have prepared it, pass it through the printer.

Photocopy printed onto Vilene with singe marks scored into it.

Marbling on fabric

Fabric paints are dropped onto water that has been thickened with floater powder. The colours spread out and are then drawn into the powder, creating swirling patterns. The fabric is then gently lowered onto the surface and lifted off after a few seconds. I have the seen this technique demonstrated on Lutradur, nylon organza and acrylic felt with perfectly clear marbling results.

Background: marbling technique on Lutradur, done for me by Craig Joubert, who was demonstrating the technique at the Knitting and Stitching Show. Foreground: Lutradur with oval apertures and a paper-bag design transferred onto it.

Gesso

Change the surface of nylon organza from shiny to matt by brushing a thin coat of gesso over it. (Cheap quality gesso is perfectly adequate for this.)

Working with gesso

Place a piece of nylon organza on a piece of plastic sheeting and brush over it with one coating of gesso. If you hold the two bottom corners and lift it off the plastic slowly and squarely, then pin it up to dry by those corners, the coating should be perfectly evenly textured. If you're not too worried about a bit of unevenness of texture, then just lift it off the plastic and pin it up to dry.

There will be sufficient gesso left on the plastic to coat another piece and it's always a good idea to prepare several pieces at the same time. Try using it on other fabrics; alternatively, substitute acrylic paints for the gesso. See also the mark-making on page 39, the book cover on page 85 and the background on pages 112–115.

Paper-bag transfer printing

The printed patterns on some paper bags can be transferred onto fabric to give instant backgrounds on which to work. It's a good idea to protect your ironing board with baking parchment to prevent it from also being printed with the design. Having done this, simply place the paper bag on your fabric, with the pattern right side down, and iron over it with a hot iron. Some patterns transfer instantly, while others take a bit more time, so lift up a corner of the paper to check if the pattern is being transferred.

Other ideas

- Iron pattern over pattern as many times as you like, using the same design or a different one.
- Block-print over patterns.
- Cut shapes out of the paper bag; arrange them pattern side down on a plain or patterned fabric, and iron over them.

The design on a paper bag was transferred onto Vilene (Pellon) three times, each time changing the position, after which it was embellished with singe marks.

Block printing

Wooden printing blocks were used here, but the range of possibilities offered by this technique is endless.

Requirements
- Fabrics on which to print
- A piece of wadding or an old towel
- Sponge
- Acrylic paints
- Wooden printing blocks

Method
Place the fabric on a soft surface, such as a piece of wadding or a folded towel. Use the sponge to put an even coat of paint on the block; don't put it on too thickly. Press on the block firmly without rocking it; lift it off, and repeat the design over the fabric. Wash the block and sponge before the paint dries hard (for suppliers, see page 126).

Block-printed design on Evolon. The shapes were cut from fabrics layered in the following order:

1. A backing of black acrylic felt.
2. Vilene painted with diluted orange acrylic paints and then block-printed.
3. A block print on Evolon, with small areas of the design cut out.
4. Fine lines scored in the design to reveal the strong orange colour beneath and at the same time fuse the layers together.
5. The layers were then cut into square tiles, rearranged and fused onto a backing of Vilene onto which the print from a paper bag had been transferred.

Adding colour to Vilene (Pellon)

Use a sponge to dampen the surface of the Vilene, then brush
or sponge diluted acrylic paints or Brusho over it so that the
colours mingle together. Dry with a hairdryer.

For the background,
Bondaweb was ironed onto
painted Vilene/spunbond
fabric. Shapes were cut
from a second piece of
printed Vilene/spunbond
fabric, then ironed onto the
background. Piece by Kim
Thittichai.

Beads made with Vilene

Most of you will have made beads out of paper or fabric before. If so, you may have found that when you are winding the fabric it slips and the windings become loose. Using the following method, in which you fuse the layers together as you wind them around the knitting needle, prevents this from happening and the finished beads are very strong and evenly shaped.

Requirements

- Basic tools and equipment
- Vilene (Pellon) (I block-printed it first)
- Card template
- A metal knitting needle

Method

1. Place the Vilene right side down, with the template on top. Draw around it with a pencil and then draw several more shapes.
2. Place the Vilene on the glass and use the ruler and the soldering iron to cut out the shapes by scoring along the lines.
3. Place one shape right side down on the glass, with the widest end nearest to you. Make a 6mm (¼in) fold at this end and then place your ruler horizontally, just in from the folded edge, and run the tip of the soldering iron along to make three or four tiny running-stitch marks to fuse the fold down, forming a channel through which the knitting needle will fit tightly (see diagram).
4. Push the needle through the channel.
5. Wind the fabric firmly around the needle then, after a couple of turns, push the tip of the soldering iron through the layers and make a short running-stitch mark to fuse them together. Continue winding and fusing the layers together after every one or two turns.
6. As the bead gets fatter, make the mark deeper into the layers to make the bead stronger. Make sure the mark is always covered by the next turn of fabric. On the last layer, push the tip of the soldering iron through several layers to make a row of evenly spaced tiny decorative eyelets all around the middle of the bead.
7. If necessary, before slipping the bead off the needle, just lightly run the tip of the soldering iron around both ends to neaten them.

The template for beads shows the end folded over and basted down with running-stitch marks.

Interlinked Vilene circles

Assembly

1. Cut three circles from painted Vilene (Pellon). Make cuts in each circle as in the three diagrams. The cuts should be as wide as the thickness of the Vilene.
2. Fit slot A of circle 1 into slot A of circle 2, with slot B of circle 2 uppermost.
3. Slide slot A of circle 3 down into slot B of circle 2. Open out slot A of circle 3 so that each half slides into slots B and C of circle 1.
4. Gently manipulate and push down on circle 3 until slots B of circles 1 and 3 and slots C of circles 1 and 3 engage.

CIRCLE 1

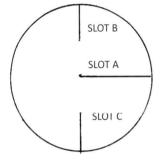

- SLOT A goes to the centre
- SLOT B and C go halfway

CIRCLE 2

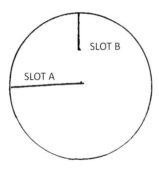

- SLOT A goes to the centre
- SLOT B goes halfway

CIRCLE 3

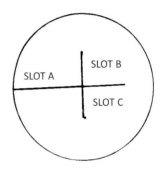

- Slot A goes a little over three-quarters across the circle
- SLOTS B and C go halfway to the outer edge

Beads made from block-printed Vilene, and circles cut using a metal wheel template, by Andrew Beal.

Painting Bondaweb

Bondaweb (Wonder Under) has long been a favourite with creative embroiderers and whoever first thought of it deserves a big thank you. Bondaweb is an adhesive webbing, backed with silicon paper; the surface is gritty due to the adhesive, which melts when heated. It can be coloured with diluted acrylic fabric paints or Brusho and ironed onto almost any fabric or paper.

When painted Bondaweb is ironed onto acrylic felt, the surface feels almost like soft leather. Painted Bondaweb ironed onto nylon organza takes the shine off the fabric, creating a nice matt texture on which to work.

I have also ironed painted Bondaweb or plain Bondaweb onto Vilene and printed it with a photocopy of one of my designs.

Method

1. Carefully brush or paint diluted paints over the gritty surface of the Bondaweb, blending the colours together, and leave it to dry. The gritty surface will become very wrinkled.
2. Protect your ironing surface with baking parchment and place the Bondaweb painted side down on your chosen fabric. Cover the silicon paper with a sheet of baking parchment to protect your iron, which should not be in steam mode.
3. Iron over the baking parchment with a medium-to-hot iron to fuse the Bondaweb to the fabric. When it is cool, carefully peel the silicon paper away.

Friendly Plastic

Friendly Plastic is a non-toxic plastic that can be heated with the heat tool and then manipulated into shapes. Here it has been coloured with metallic paints and fused into a background of layered fabrics backed with acrylic felt and embellished with marks. For stockists of Friendly Plastic, see Suppliers, page 126.

Bondaweb was painted with diluted metallic acrylic paints and Brusho. Lots of layered apertures and motifs left over from previous projects were layered on top of one another and the painted Bondaweb was ironed over them, making an uneven, textured surface. Motifs were cut out, and the remaining fabric was placed on a backing of black lining fabric. The motifs were rearranged and fused in the apertures by running the tip of the soldering iron carefully around the edges and into the lining fabric.

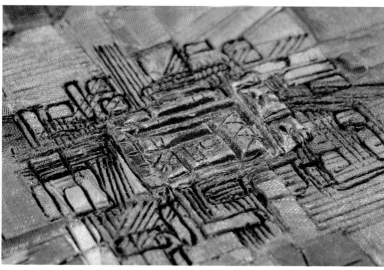

Friendly Plastic coloured with metallic paints and embedded into a background fabric.

Suppliers

UK

Margaret Beal
www.fusingfabric.co.uk
E-mail: burningissues@margaretbeal.co.uk
Tel: 01264 365102
Fine-tipped soldering irons
European and USA/Canadian soldering irons also available
Acrylic felt
Nylon organza packs of assorted colours
Packs of assorted synthetic fabrics

Christine Thomas
www.christinethomas.eu
chiaro@folksy.com
Tel: 01656 784 514
Day schools and workshops

Art van Go
www.artvango.co.uk
Tel: 01438 814946
Face masks, soldering irons, mixed-media supplies

Kim Thittichai
www.nid-noi.com
Tel: 01273 694449
Mixed media products
Vilene, Lutradur, Evolon, Bondaweb

Colouricious
Jamie Malden
www.colouricious.com
Tel: 01494 721 471
For the best range of printing blocks anywhere
DVDs, TV programmes, workshops

Molten Designs
www.theframeworkshop.co.uk
Tel: 01782 286730
Friendly Plastic, heat tools and mixed media products
Tyvek and Kunin felt

Germany

Quiltstar
www.quiltstar.de/kontakt.html
Tel: 0761-4002680
Fine-tipped soldering irons
Mixed media supplies
Nylon organza
Vilene
Lutradur
Evolon
Sizoflor

Australia

The Thread Studio
www.thethreadstudio.com
E-mail: mail@thethreadstudio.com
Tel: 08 9227 1561
Vilene
Evolon
Lutradur
Hot tools
Mixed media supplies

USA

Meinke Toy
www.meinketoy.com
Fabrics
Mixed media products

Picture credits

Pages 2, 6, 15, 29, 33, 38, 40, 41, 42, 56, 59, 66, 86, 110 (top), 113, 123, 125 (bottom) by Richard Dawson. All other photography by Michael Wicks.

Further reading

Beal, Margaret, *Fusing Fabric: Creative Cutting, Bonding and Mark making with the Soldering Iron*. Batsford, 2005

Beaney, Jan and Littlejohn, Jean, 'Double Trouble', a whole series of booklets on everything you need to know about creative embroidery and mixed-media techniques. Double Trouble Enterprises

Headley, Gwen, *Drawn to Stitch: Line, Drawing and Mark-making in Textile Art*. Batsford, 2010

Issett, Ruth, *Print, Pattern and Colour*. Batsford, 2007

Morrell, Anne, *The Techniques of Indian Embroidery*. Batsford, 1994.

Neich, Roger and Pendergrast, Mick, *Traditional Tapa Textiles of the Pacific*. Thames and Hudson, 1997

Thittichai, Kim, *Hot Textiles; Experimental Textiles, Layered Textiles*. Batsford, 2007, 2009 and 2011; *Creative Bondaweb* (DVD)

Two squares with slits cut into them were fused together back to back to form three-dimensional diamond shapes. See pages 98–99.

Index

Vilene painted over with an almost dry brush and then block printed.